Marketization

Marketization

*How Capitalist Exchange Disciplines Workers
and Subverts Democracy*

Ian Greer and Charles Umney

BLOOMSBURY ACADEMIC
LONDON • NEW YORK • OXFORD • NEW DELHI • SYDNEY

BLOOMSBURY ACADEMIC
Bloomsbury Publishing Plc
50 Bedford Square, London, WC1B 3DP, UK
1385 Broadway, New York, NY 10018, USA
29 Earlsfort Terrace, Dublin 2, Ireland

BLOOMSBURY, BLOOMSBURY ACADEMIC and the Diana logo are trademarks
of Bloomsbury Publishing Plc

First published in Great Britain 2022

Series design by Adriana Brioso

A catalogue record for this book is available from the British Library.

Library of Congress Cataloging-in-Publication Data

Names: Greer, Ian (Writer on industrial relations), author. | Umney, Charles, author.
Title: Marketization : how capitalist exchange subverts democracy and disciplines workers /
Ian Greer and Charles Umney.
Description: London ; New York : Bloomsbury Academic, 2022. |
Includes bibliographical references.
Identifiers: LCCN 2022020320 (print) | LCCN 2022020321 (ebook) | ISBN 9781913441463
(paperback) | ISBN 9781913441456 (hardback) | ISBN 9781913441425 (epub) |
ISBN 9781913441449 (pdf) | ISBN 9781350296855
Subjects: LCSH: Labor market–Europe. | Employment agencies–Europe.
Classification: LCC HD5914.A6 G73 2022 (print) | LCC HD5914.A6 (ebook) |
DDC 331.12094–dc23/eng/20220512
LC record available at https://lccn.loc.gov/2022020320
LC ebook record available at https://lccn.loc.gov/2022020321

ISBN: HB: 978-1-9134-4145-6
PB: 978-1-9134-4146-3
ePDF: 978-1-9134-4144-9
eBook: 978-1-9134-4142-5

Typeset by Deanta Global Publishing Services, Chennai, India
Printed and bound in Great Britain

To find out more about our authors and books visit www.bloomsbury.com and sign up
for our newsletters.

Contents

Acknowledgements

This book reports on a research project, the core of which was travelling around Europe and conversing, pre-pandemic and therefore normally in-person. This included one-on-one interviews with dozens of non-academic experts – musicians, healthcare professionals, social workers, managers, policymakers, trade unionists and other kinds of activists – who we cannot name because we promised them anonymity and confidentiality. We thank these interviewees for allowing us to invite ourselves into the places where they work, taking the time to speak to us and contributing their knowledge. We hope that they recognize their own stories in the text.

Much of the conversation was with our students and fellow academics. The most intensive interactions were with the marketization research team at the University of Greenwich, which was in place from about 2012 to 2016, including Geneviève Coderre-Lapalme, Nick Krachler, Lefteris Kretsos, Maria Mantynen, Maria Alejandra Rodriguez, Barbara Samaluk, Lisa Schulte, Shanaz Sumra and Graham Symon. They also include others who co-authored books and papers with us based on this and related work, including Jennie Auffenberg, Dario Azzelini, Karen Breidahl, Nils Böhlke, Sue Corby, David Hall, Marco Hauptmeier, Katia Iankova, Matthias Knuth, Flemming Larsen, Jane Lethbridge, Nathan Lillie, Wenceslas Lizé, Özlem Onaran and Thorsten Schulten. We also thank those who carried out commissioned work on our projects: Rolle Alho, Uli Brinkmann, Erka Caro, Stefanie Hürtgen, Andy Morton, Oliver Nachtwey, Elisa Panini, Engelbert Stockhammer, Pete Turnbull and Antti Turtainen. Thanks to other participants in workshops organized by the team in Berlin (2012), Greenwich (2013, 2014, 2015), Ithaca (2015), Konnevesi (2014), Leeds (2015) and Ljubljana (2015). Thanks also to participants in pandemic-era webinar discussions of the manuscript at the British Sociological Association conference (in 2020) and organized by academic friends in Leeds and Strathclyde (both in early 2021), as well as an in-person discussion at the Society for the Advancement of Socio-Economics in Amsterdam (in summer 2022).

Other important contributors did not work directly on the marketization-related projects. Ian thanks Ginny Doellgast for daily conversations about these issues, Mark Stuart for support during the development of the basic idea at Leeds, Ian Greenwood for opening doors early on in the UK, Jon Sibson for mentorship on the practicalities of marketization and management at Greenwich and Harry Katz for the time and space at Cornell to finish the project. Others have said things to us that shaped our decisions about this book, including Alexandre Afonso, Rose Batt, Klaus Dörre, Xavier Dumay, Jerôme Gautié, Chris Howell, Gregory Jackson, Damian Grimshaw, Lena Hipp, Chris Howell, Karen Jaehrling, Chris Kai-Jones, Jörg Sydow, Dieter Plehwe, Lowell Turner, Matt Vidal and Kyoung-Hee Yu. Some of the above-mentioned people also commented on drafts of this book, as did Jens Arnholtz, Sundeep Aulakh, Dario Azzellini, Chiara Benassi, Thierry Berthet, Nadja Cirulies, Matt Cole, Stefano Gasparri, Marco Hauptmeier, Miguel Martinez Lucio, Bjarke Refslund, Jay Wiggan and an anonymous reviewer.

The largest funder for our marketization research has been the European Research Council (The Effects of Marketization on Societies #313613). Another substantial grant came from the Hans Böckler Foundation (the Marketization of Employment Services in European Comparison), which also provided a smaller grant (Online Platforms and Worker Representation in Live Music). Also feeding into this book were smaller projects with the Public and Commercial Services Union and the European Foundation for the Improvement of Living and Working Conditions, as well as small grants from Leeds University and the University of Greenwich.

Finally, we thank our family members who have supported us during the research and writing of this book, especially Susie Ioannou and Ginny Doellgast.

Part I

A theory of marketization

The political economy of marketization

What is the relationship between capitalism and markets? Sometimes, they are offhandedly portrayed as more or less the same thing, as when Leszek Kołakowski (2005: 12–13) writes that 'Communism in its Leninist-Stalinist version seems to have been crushed. "Capitalism" – i.e., the market – seems to be continuing its triumphant conquest of the world.' Sometimes, as in classical Marxist thought, capitalist elites are presumed to suppress markets over time by forming giant monopolies that stifle competition. For other writers, markets are an overwhelming force that put pressure on societies and the people within them to participate in the capitalist system. Politicians routinely justify market-centric policies on the grounds that 'there is no alternative' other than to make a national economy 'competitive' and bolster 'market confidence'.

The subject of this book is not 'markets' in general, or 'the market', whatever that means, but 'marketization'. By this, we mean the concrete processes through which market competition is created, intensified, extended and maintained in the real world, whether through the strategic decisions of private businesses or by governments looking to reform public services. Mainstream economists often treat markets as fundamental to the human condition, based on the view that it is natural for individuals to seek to exchange and barter with others to maximize their own advantage. But if that were the case, marketization would be a simple matter of allowing people to do what they would do anyway, of removing obstacles and letting individuals do the rest. In practice, stimulating competition is easier said than done. Marketization frequently involves awkward bureaucratic manoeuvring, the creation of new institutions, processes, rules and incentives, as well as higher costs. The people affected by it often do what they can to resist it or protect themselves from it, in some cases having to be persuaded quite forcefully to go along with the new way of doing things. Despite all the problems that come with marketization, the principle of creating and extending price-based competition has become an increasingly important feature of European political economy.

Let us consider a real-world example to show what we mean. Anglophone comparative scholars normally treat Germany as the type of capitalist economy where collective bargaining and other worker protections limit the extent and effects of market competition. But this is not what we saw in our travels in Germany, which began almost twenty years ago. In autumn 2003, the powerful metalworkers' union IG Metall had just been defeated in its efforts to reduce working time in East Germany to thirty-five hours, which would have meant a rise in hourly pay rates to the same level as in the West. Employers had responded by threatening to move work to lower-cost countries, claiming that equalizing pay would compromise competitiveness and risk further job loss.

Simultaneously, the centre–left coalition government was implementing the so-called Hartz reforms, which reduced unemployment insurance benefits for most workers, permitted new kinds of part-time and temporary jobs, and ratcheted up pressures on the unemployed to look for work, including financial penalties for those who turned down job offers. In a country where egalitarian pay scales and secure jobs were supposedly the norm, low wages and temporary jobs – agency work, mini-jobs and one-Euro jobs – were proliferating. Through all these developments, driven both by government and by corporate actors, German political economy was being altered in a way that greatly extended the influence of principles of market competition.

While the workers we met in Germany were often profoundly concerned about these developments, many academic experts told us they were nothing to worry about. Marketization was not a problem. The government, they pointed out, was still a centre–left coalition. They claimed that the most important business associations and employers still saw the German model of social partnership as a comparative advantage that would not simply be sacrificed at the altar of the market. They argued that the East German metalworking employers that had gone to war with the union were exceptions, not the rule. Trade union membership was declining, but collective bargaining and works councils remained in place, protecting most German workers. The growth in poor-quality service sector jobs was a lesser evil than people leaving the labour market and receiving unemployment benefits. According to the conventional thinking of the 1990s, any job was better than no job, precarious (or 'flexible') employment could be expanded without undermining the collective bargaining system and, above all, the chief instrument to expand employment should be 'the market' (Streeck and Heinze, 1999).

Later it would become evident that these reforms coincided with a significant rise in poverty, income inequality and low-wage work in Germany (Bosch and Weinkopf, 2008; OECD, 2008). Correlation, of course, does not equal causation, and a range of factors are needed to explain these statistical trends. But credible threats of offshoring and outsourcing, the rollback of unemployment insurance, the privatization of public services, the liberalization of temporary jobs and increased hostility to trade unions by employers undoubtedly made it more difficult for German workers to get a better deal from their employers while helping the latter to restructure in response to market pressures.

In the UK, a similar process was enacted, albeit using different tools and a different timeframe. By undermining collective bargaining systems and weakening trade unions through a flurry of legislation during the 1980s, the UK government made it far more difficult for British workers to negotiate better deals and mitigate the impact of the business cycle on pay and working conditions. This helps to explain why British wages have been so slow to recover from the financial crisis of 2007 (Machin, 2015).

The same is true of many European countries. These were the kinds of changes that the institutions of the European Union were encouraging in an ever-growing number of member states – they pushed countries to make it easier for employers to reshape working conditions and job security as they saw fit, while making it harder for workers to collectively contest these decisions. We call this process 'class discipline'. This book is motivated by our intuition that marketization has been an important means of instilling class discipline across European societies.

Capitalism is not the same as marketization. Capitalism is a mode of production that is organized around the accumulation of privately owned capital, with corresponding capitalist states and institutions that take pains to enable this kind of accumulation on an ever-expanding scale. In a capitalist economic system, production is usually carried out by workers who do not own the enterprises where they work, but whose living depends on wages paid by capitalists. The goods and services produced under capitalism are then exchanged in virtual or physical marketplaces. The need to compete against other capitalists to successfully recoup investment by selling in the marketplace is a constant pressure. Market competition can push capitalists to produce more efficiently, tighten control over their workers or innovate. In theory, intensified competition makes it harder for them to generate profits.

Hence, the term 'the market' is sometimes used to refer to a simplified picture of individuals freely competing to buy and sell commodities at whichever prices they negotiate. Irrespective of whether the free market is seen to unleash potential in ways that are fundamental to the human condition or as an ineffective, inequitable and self-serving idea promoted by billionaires and modelled by economists, 'the market' itself is normally seen in simplified and abstracted form. But our objective is to examine the concrete ways in which market competition is created and managed in practice. Who 'marketizes'? And how?

Various things are necessary to successfully create and intensify market exchange:

(1) The things being exchanged need to be made readily comparable. There needs to be some way of quantifying the value of a given good or service that can inform a monetary price. In other

words, the thing being exchanged needs to be commoditized. Without this, prices are difficult to set and competition cannot happen smoothly. For example, judging the value of different live musicians is clearly highly subjective, but if a company can set up a website that allows different acts to be ranked according to customer-generated star ratings, then there is a firmer basis for competition.

(2) The competitive arena needs to become open to new buyers or sellers who wish to take part. Without openness, the outcomes of exchange can be stitched up in advance and real competition eliminated. For example, competition to provide patient scans on behalf of a hospital may stagnate if only one or two companies are prepared to do it, or if public authorities prioritize their existing contacts. To have real competition, more providers need to be encouraged into the marketplace.

(3) Transactions have to occur frequently. With infrequent transactions, competition stalls. For example, if a contract to provide welfare-to-work services to disadvantaged populations lasts five years, competitive pressure on the organization providing it is much less intense than if they have to compete for more work every twelve months.

Marketization, in this book, refers to the real-world mechanisms through which the process of exchange is reorganized – whether by governments or by businesses – to bring these conditions about. There is no 'pure' marketization, where all these processes are implemented fully; there is always room for improvement if the goal is more commodification, openness and speed. But these are rarely the only goals for the parties involved, as we shall see. Workers and citizens often find effective ways of resisting and obstructing marketization, and the government agencies and capitalists who implement marketization are usually wary of losing control.

Effective class discipline may require measured doses of marketization, rather than an all-out push. Indeed, we will argue that there is no contradiction between monopolies and marketization. Firms that dominate marketplaces can use their dominance to unleash marketization processes on their workers or on firms in their supply chains; this is what online platforms sometimes accomplish. Similarly, public-sector entities often create 'quasi-markets', in which they are the only buyers and have to design the market. Monopolists (or oligopolists) can thus be marketizers, because they have the power to determine the terms on which market competition is conducted.

Marketization does not happen easily or automatically, and there are circumstances where it might seem to be highly unlikely to happen at all. Here, we will identify situations where investors, managers, workers, policymakers and others have a strong interest in limiting some or all of the three aspects of marketization. Despite this, marketization has proven profoundly attractive in European capitalist societies, not only for neoliberal true believers but also for more practically minded experts and elites who have absorbed the view that the market is fairer and more efficient than the alternatives.

We argue that marketization, in the context of current European political economy, takes the form it does because of its role in imposing class discipline. By class discipline, we mean any measures which make it harder for workers to negotiate with their employers to improve working conditions, pay and job security, and easier for capitalists to make decisions about these issues unilaterally. Marketization is in many cases motivated by the desire to instil class discipline, and, therefore, increased class discipline is frequently an intended consequence of marketization initiatives. Consider the German workers we mentioned earlier. They faced threats of offshoring, outsourcing or privatization; their unemployment benefits became more meagre and punitive, and they had to compete with a growing pool of insecure or underemployed workers. Their employers were increasingly competing on an international scale or against other subcontracting firms. Even public-sector workers were told they had to compete with the private sector. This competition was invoked as a justification when workers were required to accept lower wages and insecure employment contracts.

Workers accepted concessions demanded by employers in part because the Hartz reforms had made the prospect of job loss increasingly frightening, since the welfare state would no longer protect their income, skills and status through periods of unemployment (Brinkmann et al., 2006). In sum, various measures converged, all of which intensified market pressures on workers themselves, which in turn forced them to accept the worsening of their conditions of employment.[1]

Certainly, the idea of competition as the solution to the world's problems is not part of the Zeitgeist in the same way as it was when we started this work. The political right has produced deeply illiberal figures like Donald Trump and Viktor Orbán, who do not appear to be true believers in open markets. Believers in the benign powers of 'the market' still discuss the dangers of restricting competition, and their examples point to concentrated corporate power enabled by government (Philippon, 2019). The centre–left has rallied around causes like Me Too and Black Lives Matter, which question the manifold injustices of the neoliberal era and some of its main ideological underpinnings. In the wake of the Covid-19 pandemic, governments have sharply restricted economic activity (and freedom) while attempting to coordinate massive vaccination programmes and vastly (if temporarily) expanding the size of the welfare state through furlough schemes and the like, seemingly a rebuttal of the market. It is no longer fashionable to rhapsodize about market forces as a panacea for social problems, nor is neoliberalism the pre-eminent target of radical critique that it once was.

Nevertheless, marketization is not going away. The market mechanisms we observed are still embedded in European political economy and will likely remain so even in the wake of the economic and social convulsions caused by the Covid-19 pandemic. Whether in services to assist the unemployed, healthcare or live music (the three examples we discuss in some depth), even genuine cataclysms

---

[1] In the language of academic labour studies, marketization weakens the structural power resources of workers by making it harder for them to disrupt production (see Silver, 2003; and Schmalz et al., 2018).

have failed to prompt large-scale alternatives. Before we outline how pervasive marketization has become in European political economy in recent decades, we will briefly describe our research.

Studying marketization

At this point, we need to issue a warning: our account of marketization and its effects takes us to some tangled and, frankly, infuriating places. Unlike Marx, who invites readers of *Capital* to the factory floor, we poke around in the offices where business strategy and government policy are made. These include the agencies responsible for 'commissioning', 'procurement' or 'purchasing' and the administrative corridors of hospitals, job centres, municipalities, ministries and the European Commission.

The book will not appeal to optimists and self-styled pragmatists. We do not tell edifying stories of governments using the power of markets to improve the world, and we travel well outside of our intellectual comfort zone to find out how these markets work. Observing the work of marketizers in Europe requires entering the unhappy fog of bureaucratic confusion and perverse incentives. Our intention has been to arrive at an interpretation of European political economy that is grounded in the everyday life of market participants.

Our research was interview-based. In the countries we visited, we held in-depth discussions with as many people as we could in the sectors we studied – hospitals, welfare-to-work systems and live music. For our five-country marketization study, 225 individuals were interviewed, our three-country employment services study included 114 additional interviews and our follow-up study on online platforms in live music involved fifteen interviews, in addition to previous waves of interviews conducted with thirty British live musicians. (We will draw most heavily on material from Great Britain, Germany, France and Brussels, but it will be evident that we also have looked at Denmark, Finland, Greece and Slovenia.) The vast majority of these interviews were carried out by one or both of us, and the vast majority of those carried out by other members of the project teams were documented in a way that allowed us to use them as data for our publications. Interviewees included workers and trade unionists, public administrators, employers and industry lobbyists, and practitioner-researchers (who are particularly numerous in healthcare). Rather than seeking out a sample representative of particular population groups, we were in most cases looking for key informants, that is, people who had a wealth of insider knowledge based on the professional or bureaucratic niches they occupied and whom we could interrogate about the inner workings of marketization initiatives.

The advantage of our approach was that we could get a closer look at the bureaucratic mechanics of marketization than if, say, we analysed quantitative data about a particular marketization process and its effects. This meant that we could speak to the policymakers who designed marketization measures about their motivations and methods. We could then speak with the public administrators and private contractors charged with implementing policy change. And we also talked to front-line workers and their representatives (such as trade union reps) about how the nature of their work was changing.

This was not an easy process. It was often difficult to puzzle out who the right person to speak to was who understood the particular parts of the case we needed, and people were not always keen to talk to us. Snowball sampling – for example where project partners referred us to interviewees, who then referred us to their professional contacts – was sometimes effective. But this was also sometimes inappropriate, because the knowledge we needed was not always present in the networks where we already had contacts. Scientific objectivity required us to cold-call experts, show up uninvited at offices and strike up conversations at demonstrations or industry events.

Our method allows us to trace the consequences of marketization policies through different contexts and bureaucratic levels, examining how they evolved in practice and how their effects rippled outwards. It also sheds light on the barriers to marketization. Some of our most important interviews, for example, were with private-sector managers who expressed their belief in the potential power of privatization and marketization, their frustrations about interactions with public authorities or trade unionists and the impediments they experienced to profit-making. We drew insights from comparing these conversations with those we had had with other people including front-line workers, slowly developing an understanding of complicated systems where most people seemed unhappy with how marketization measures were panning out but for very different reasons. The aim was to develop a critical theory of marketization grounded in empirical study of particular markets in capitalist societies across Europe.

Marketization in European integration

The context of our research is Europe from the 1980s up to 2016. During this period, an ever-increasing number of countries recast their institutions around the objective of a single market. We were based in London and Leeds, but our research took us to Brussels, Denmark, Finland, France, Germany, Greece and Slovenia. The research started in 2003, but many interviewees explained their situation in light of the events of the 1980s and 1990s: Thatcher's neoliberal reforms, the collapse of the Soviet Bloc, the single market and the creation of the Euro. As our research progressed, the EU expanded to include a dozen new accession countries, most of them post-Socialist, and there was a global financial crisis. Just after our research ended, the UK voted to leave the EU in a repudiation of one of the main pillars of the European integration project, the free movement of people.

Marketization has been a central feature of European integration. Already in 1957, the basic principles were enshrined in the Treaty of Rome, including freedom of movement of goods, services, capital and labour between member states of the European Economic Community. Over the decades, eliminating barriers to these freedoms, such as tariffs, immigration restrictions, capital controls and border checkpoints, was one side of this project. The other side was introducing new domestic arrangements to facilitate exchange across borders. A common currency, the privatization and re-regulation of industries like energy, transportation and telecommunications, mutual recognition of social security arrangements and the enforcement of transparency and equal treatment in public procurement were all ways that the EU sought to grease the wheels of exchange through transforming the domestic institutions of its member states. In the 1990s these measures intensified in the wake of the Maastricht Treaty, which spelled out certain market-making policies (like the Euro, intended to accelerate cross-border transactions). Meanwhile, changes to governance processes helped to overcome resistance to new market-centric policies (like qualified majority voting in the Council of Ministers).

To gain some understanding of the ramifications of marketization in Europe, consider worker posting. Under the free movement of services, employers operating across different member states could deploy their workers by 'posting' them to various countries. This raised a serious problem for the trade union movement, since wages, social insurance costs and working conditions vary between countries. Working with Nathan Lillie in Germany, Great Britain and Finland, we examined this in construction, the main industry that employed posted workers, and found that firms were taking advantage of worker posting to reduce their costs and skim off surpluses, normally using complex webs of corporate entities (Lillie and Greer, 2007).

Unions were not well positioned to respond. On one construction site we visited in Britain, a group of Hungarian workers were employed by an Austrian contractor through a Hungarian subsidiary that functioned as a labour-only subcontractor. In another case, group of Polish workers on a site in Finland were paid Polish wage levels, but unknown to them were employed by a Cyprus-based firm paying Cypriot payroll taxes. In Germany at this time, contractors were using posted workers against a backdrop of mass unemployment in construction, leading to a dramatic decline in union membership and weakening of its ability to collectively bargain. Not only did these unions face a new group of hyper-mobile workers who they did not know how to organize, but they also faced the difficult question of how to enforce workplace standards without victimizing migrants. Working with law enforcement (an important part of the German union's strategy) and mobilizing large protests at the sites (which happened repeatedly in Britain) could be counterproductive if the goal was to organize migrants into the union. The best-known example was a strike at the Lindsey oil refinery in Lincolnshire, where workers ostensibly protesting to improve wages and conditions for Italian posted workers brought signs demanding 'British jobs for British workers' (invoking a slogan used by the then prime minister, Gordon Brown).

Worker posting also illustrates some controversies built into European integration. Firms based in low-wage countries were undercutting competitors in higher-wage countries using lower wages and social security contributions. As Magdalena Bernaciak (2015) points out, this was not simply a matter of 'social dumping', in which low-wage countries were using lower labour standards to take jobs away from workers in higher-wage countries. General contractors based in high-wage countries were active players, like the Austrian contractor mentioned earlier, who were pushing down their costs using subcontractors from low-wage countries (often without legal liability for violations of workers' rights by subcontractors). If governments passed laws, or workers boycotted and shut down a construction site, to stop this race to the bottom, aren't they violating the basic freedoms of the EU? In the 1996 Worker Posting Directives, EU law came to recognize certain legal minima that countries could impose, such as minimum wages. But in the so-called Laval Quartet of decisions that followed this, the Court of Justice of the European Union (CJEU) ruled that countries would have to balance labour rights and social protections against the freedom of movement of services. The former would have to avoid obstructing the latter (Koukiadaki, 2014).

Although the 2018 Worker Posting Directive created a stronger basis for member states to ensure equal pay for equal work, these controversies exposed how market freedoms have trumped social protection in the process of European integration. As Fritz Scharpf noted already in the

1990s, the decision-making process of the EU was far better suited for pushing liberalization than for improving social protections (Scharpf, 1999). While the former could be driven effectively from the centre, the latter requires more tailoring. A policy that may raise standards in one country may lower them in another; this is why Nordic countries, with the support of unions and centre–left parties, tend to obstruct EU-level social standards, such as a coordinated minimum wage (Bender and Kjellberg, 2021).

The problem is not that EU integration lacks a social dimension. It has social policies and enforceable labour standards built into directives covering working time, health and safety, equality rules, the coordination of social security systems and the protection of patients in health systems. Beyond this, EU institutions have sought to build on binding standards using 'soft law'. By promoting the notion of 'flexicurity', for example, EU institutions have encouraged member states not only to give employers more freedom to hire and fire but also to compensate workers through investments in training and unemployment benefits.

The problem is the asymmetry between social protection and marketization. Social policies and labour protections are subordinate or reactive to market-making policy and have less of a solid anchoring in EU treaties and institutions. And, with the rising power of the European Central Bank (ECB), social policy has also been reshaped in another way, through the enforcement of austerity and fiscal discipline, which has checked the expansion of government-funded social benefits, services or jobs. The consequence is that policies to promote flexibility for capital develop more quickly than those to promote security for workers, leading to inequality and precarity (Hürtgen, 2021). While it is true that member states have found new ways to regulate worker posting that conform to the rules of the single market (Refslund et al., 2020), this has taken place after the damage was already done.

There is little in the way of democratic oversight by the European public that could overcome this. Elected leaders of member states negotiate over treaties and determine the priorities of key institutions like the Commission, but EU policymaking is so opaque that it is difficult for voters to punish their elected officials for unpopular EU-level policies. Proponents of European integration live in fear of referenda in member states, because empowering voters increases the risk that their agenda will face setbacks. But more importantly, independence from 'politics' is an important part of how the main EU institutions are supposed to work. According to this principle, the Commission should develop new directives and guidelines in line with instructions from the member states, the CJEU should make rulings based on the EU's directives and the ECB should govern the money supply in line with its prerogative to maintain price stability, all without 'political' interference (e.g. from voters or their elected representatives).

During the 1930s, Friedrich Hayek (1980) (perhaps the most important inspiration for today's believers in the free market) anticipated this asymmetry. He argued that an interstate federation to promote free trade through shared economic governance would serve as a valuable check on socialism within member countries. The international market would punish democratic governments that chose to raise taxes or wages, because they would become uncompetitive and suffer from capital flight. Although Hayek later became a critic of the bureaucracy behind the common market, contemporary neoliberals have come to appreciate its results. Economist Thomas Philipon's recent critique of US telecommunications policy points out that the United States has failed where Europe has succeeded, namely in promoting competition between telecommunications providers and low prices for consumers (Philipon, 2019). Effects on jobs and wages for telecommunications workers are conveniently ignored (see Doellgast, 2012). What Hayek emphasized and Philipon plays down is the central importance of insulating the key decisions about market government from 'politics' or democratic oversight.

The intervention of EU institutions in support of marketization can be very direct, as the Greek people learned during the last financial crisis. A heavily indebted government negotiated with a 'troika' of institutions – the Commission, the ECB and the International

Monetary Fund – representing the holders of Greek government debt, mainly French and German banks. As their society was in free fall, with a growing share of the population destitute and the number of suicides increasing, the government faced the threat of being kicked out of the Eurozone and possibly the European Union. Unwilling to face the prospect of 'Grexit', the left-wing Syriza government agreed to reduce public spending and minimum wages, privatize infrastructure and curtail collective bargaining rights, among other concessions. The government thus agreed to transfer income and assets to its creditors – and to local capitalists – to stave off an even deeper social and economic collapse that would likely have followed had the troika followed through on their threats.

Why have the gains of economic growth under the single market not been more equitably distributed? Heterodox economists have pointed at factors like austerity policies and financialization (Lapavitsas, 2013; Stockhammer and Onaran, 2013). We will discuss this further, but our central focus is on other aspects of market governance that more rarely attract public attention. We chose to study marketization specifically in Europe because the European integration process was so biased towards making markets. Because of the challenges of studying markets, however, it was difficult to say how widespread the marketization phenomenon really was or how much of an impact it was having. The most useful comparative study showed Germany near the top of the international league table in terms of overall liberalization policies (Höpner et al., 2011). And there is a vast literature now on the spread of neoliberal ideas in politics, institutions and everyday life around Europe (Mirowski and Plehwe, 2015). But studies of liberalization policies and neoliberal ideas do not normally tell us how concrete processes of marketization are implemented and experienced in workplaces and in front-line public services. Few marketization examples can be inferred from high-level government policy or neoliberal ideas. To identify them, a focus on everyday life is needed.

At the outset of our research, we suspected that marketization mattered, not only because EU institutions and changes to domestic policies tended to encourage it but also because our initial studies in Germany showed that it could disrupt worker protections, especially collective bargaining. In our qualitative research, we observed intensified price-based competition as a driver of this institutional erosion not only in construction but also in manufacturing, healthcare and social services. Healthcare and social services were particularly interesting, because of policies such as privatization and competitive tendering, where government was in effect disrupting its own mechanisms for social protection. But we also observed another face of marketization: a bureaucratic realm of complex and often deliberately depoliticized policymaking where the details of the market's functioning are decided.

The Goldilocks theory of state and market

It is common for pro-market critics of government to describe the EU as a case of regulatory overstretch by a supranational state, implying that a true believer in free markets should oppose it. Although utopian free marketeers dream of 'small government', the fact remains that EU regulatory expansion has enabled market competition on a scale that was previously hard to imagine. In their efforts to add a social dimension to an ever more competitive single market, EU institutions have subordinated the former to the latter.

This failure to comprehend the market-making powers of EU institutions reflects a problem in the way in which political and journalistic debates discuss the relationship between markets and state regulation. Discussions about the role of 'the market' in society frequently rely on what we will call a 'Goldilocks' view. This is the idea that state regulation and the market are two opposites, both of which are needed to some degree, and the aim is to find some kind of 'balance' between them which is just right, like Baby Bear's porridge. Eminent commentators in mainstream political economy endorse this view. Ian Bremmer (2011), for instance, depicts a 'war between the state and corporations', based on this state-market sliding scale. At one end are cases where the state does too much. These countries are bureaucratic and unfree. At the other end are countries that have too much market and not enough state. These are dangerously anarchic. Bremmer says the aim should be to find a happy midpoint where the state does enough to ensure stability but doesn't encroach on market freedoms.

Much political-economic argument accepts this sliding scale metaphor; debates take place over where along the scale the appropriate balance can be found. Right-wing 'libertarian' thought, for instance, has portrayed any interference in individual market freedoms as the start of a slippery slope towards tyrannical state control. Democratic institutions are suspect, since they might incubate this kind of agenda, for instance, by creating ever-expanding politically popular tax-funded health and welfare systems. Robert Nozick (1974), for example, advocated the 'minimal state', in which the state limits itself to preventing people from robbing and killing each other. Any more is too much, any less is too little.

Common on the liberal left is a belief that we currently have slightly too much market, meaning more state regulation is needed in the interests of equity and stability. Soft-left Goldilocks theorists may view marketization as an ideological blunder which threatens the stability of capitalism (with the latter being presumed to be worth preserving). Will Hutton (2012), for instance, advocates a 'new balance between state, business and society' where the necessary risks of the market are accompanied by regulatory safety nets. Paul Krugman exemplifies this view using the mixed metaphor of an engine that needs a safety net: 'I believe that you let markets mostly run themselves – You have an economy that's basically driven by market forces, but you collect taxes to provide a safety net.'[2]

Intellectuals and academics in the social-democratic tradition avoid these metaphors while adopting different ones. For Karl Polanyi, markets were not the opposite of the state at all: he argued that they

---

[2] This is from a TV appearance by Krugmann, which is cited in Ozimek (2012).

have to be created and planned in ways that often involve government intervention. In documenting how this happens, he provided a welcome but often unheeded pre-emptive rebuttal to the Goldilocks view. Instead, he anticipated a pendulum swing between not the state and market but society and market. Societies tend to react when land, labour and money are treated as commodities and therefore subjected to market forces. When this happens there will be some kind of countermovement which re-asserts societal control over market competition.

This might be interpreted in a naively optimistic way that rules out the possibility of markets as a destructive force but could also be understood more subtly. For contemporary Polanyians, for instance, the point is that, wherever governing institutions create new instances of market competition, we will also tend to see overlapping changes that 're-embed' market forces in new forms of regulation. This may be through the creation of new non-market institutions or changes in the wider social and political landscape. The ways in which this happens are likely to be unexpected, spontaneous and much less 'planned' than marketization itself (Streeck and Thelen, 2005). Hence, the most important tension is between the society (not the state) and the market. Modern Polanyians such as Mariana Mazzucato, have gone so far as to argue that the Goldilocks view of state and market as opposites is an intellectual blunder that lies at the heart of many of the world's political-economic problems. Instead, an 'entrepreneurial state' is required that creates markets and actively takes part in them, thus infusing them with progressive incentives (LaPlane and Mazzucato, 2020).

Still others reject the idea of a historical pendulum swing between society and market, and instead focus on pragmatism and practicalities. For example, economist James Galbraith argues in his book *The Predator State* (2008) that practically minded policymakers on the left and right will tend to reject excessive market policy agendas, because they know they don't work well for 'predation' (i.e. corporate rent seeking) or for achieving most other policy objectives. Others argue that markets are effective only in specific circumstances. For example, in Varieties of Capitalism (VOC) theory (Hall and Soskice, 2001), certain countries (like the United States and the United Kingdom) derive competitive advantages from free markets, while the economic success of others (such as Germany, Japan and the Scandinavian countries) depends on non-market forms of coordination such as collective bargaining and worker participation. According to VOC, a radical extension of the market is unlikely in the latter group because it doesn't fit well with their overall model of capitalism. If non-market coordination is functional in these economies, then there's no real reason to marketize.

A better understanding of the relationship between state, society, capitalism and markets requires addressing some misconceptions. First, contra the Kołakowski quote which begins this chapter, it is misleading to conflate capitalism with markets. Already in 1910, the Marxist economist Rudolf Hilferding was arguing that it is often capitalists and not the state, which in practice set limits on the market. We will talk about him more in a later chapter. Recent studies in the Marxist tradition are returning to this theme. See, for instance, how Ashok Kumar's (2020) study of the global textiles industry reveals specific groups of capitalists combining to limit market competition to lever up their profitability and organizational stability.

Second, there is no sliding scale between the 'free' market and the state, upon which we can find some equitable balance (what we have called the Goldilocks view). This sliding scale metaphor overlooks the fact that states engineer market competition, and that an expanding market also often means more government regulation (Vogel, 1998). That will be a constant theme of this book. The sliding scale image also obscures the question of democracy. Some on the free-market right have been honest enough to acknowledge the threat democracy poses to unimpeded markets, as we saw in relation to Hayek. This rather important issue tends to be overlooked in the more wonkish debates on the liberal left, which revolve around metaphors about 'engines', 'safety nets' and so on.

Other misconceptions arise in speculations about the limits of the market. In this book, we will reject the idea that pragmatic policymakers tend to curtail the application of market mechanisms because they see them failing. In fact, they often persist in the face of failure (Umney et al., 2018). We will also reject the belief that economies with more non-market coordination tend to keep a lid on market competition (as in VOC theory). In fact, marketization has been a radical and disruptive presence in many different countries, not just 'liberal' ones.

Finally, we also criticize Polanyian approaches that juxtapose markets with some broader notion of 'society'. The argument that societies tend to react against commodification, while it may be applicable in many circumstances, is too vague. It doesn't show who initiates, shapes and benefits from marketization, people who are members of society (often prominent and powerful ones). Nor does it appreciate the ability of capital and marketizers to circumvent those forces in capitalist societies that might prevent them from shaping the market. Polanyi himself saw conflict between classes as less fundamental than the conflict between markets and society. In our theory, competing interests between different class groups is vital to understanding the causes and consequences of marketization. In Chapters 2 and 3, we will outline our central theoretical argument: marketization, as it has played out in twenty-first -century Europe, is best understood as a tool for imposing class discipline.

The institutions of neoliberalism

We are not the first to identify these problems. For many, the pervasive and increasing importance of markets is an undeniable feature contemporary life. Much of this social science literature is institutional, about the 'rules of the game'[3] in the market and how these are embedded in other social arrangements. Historically, this meant a concern with how the expansion of markets might be limited and their worst excesses

---

[3] 'Institutions' here referring to the 'rules of the game' that contain and structure economic life (North, 1981).

avoided, with a focus on contrasting countries with liberal and non-liberal institutions. Over the past fifteen years, however, research increasingly focuses on the reverse: how institutions are subverted, deconstructed or undermined to facilitate marketization.

This is an international trend, but it doesn't look the same in all countries, as comparative political economists have shown. Lucio Baccaro and Chris Howell (2011) examine how the diverse and complex changes to labour-market regulatory institutions across many different rich capitalist countries – which they label 'liberalization' – had a shared outcome. These changes increased employers' discretion, that is their ability to adjust pay, job security and other factors in response to competitive pressure, while diminishing workers' abilities to effectively negotiate on these points. Looking at France, Jonah Levy (2008) observes that, certainly, the state has indeed sought to mitigate the consequences of marketization initiatives which have gained force since the 1980s. Levy argues that this is part of a process of 'social anaesthesis' which makes marketization more bearable for populations. Social protections facilitate the expansion of marketization, with the latter defining the overall direction of change.

Often the growing influence of the market is explained with reference to neoliberalism. Sometimes neoliberalism refers to free-market ideas with an intellectual pedigree going back to the likes of Friedman, Hayek and Buchanan, as they are disseminated by think tanks and deployed in the policymaking process (Hauptmeier and Morgan, 2021; Mirowski and Plehwe, 2015). For Loïc Wacquant (2012), neoliberalism is a wider-ranging political project which uses state power to force individuals and institutions to conform to the pressures of market logic. For followers of Michel Foucault, it is an even more general 'rationality' (see Dardot and Laval, 2010, 2014) that has become dominant since the 1970s – where individuals are increasingly encouraged and required to conceive themselves as mini-entrepreneurs, no longer expecting collective social rights as citizens but competing against others for individual reward or loss. It is thus a profound change in our collective way of life.

These discussions of neoliberalism and liberalization offer an evocative depiction of epochal shifts in capitalist society. This book is less concerned with grand narratives of institutional and societal change, and more with understanding the concrete functioning of price competition. We are concerned with the market pressures on employers that translate to poor-quality jobs. Liberalizing changes in collective bargaining or employment protection legislation gives employers more discretion in principle, intensified competition can create costs and risks, which can constrain them and which they often shift onto their workers in the form of low-paid, insecure jobs. We are also concerned with the question of whether market mechanisms, once introduced, have their intended effect. We will show that, yes, marketization can indeed seem pervasive and bullying, but it can also be brittle and dysfunctional. In the next section we will outline our theory of marketization.

Marketization matters

What is marketization? How is it different from capitalism, neoliberalism, liberalization and austerity? Who imposes marketization? Why do they do so? And what are its consequences for society? This book proposes a theory of marketization in the form of some answers to these questions.

To provide a formal definition, marketization is a concrete administrative and organizational process that produces intensified competition on the basis of price. This may be the consequence of a government policy to roll back worker protections or the retreat of the state due to austerity, but it is not necessarily so. Indeed, there are more direct ways to ratchet up competition. For example, the corporate strategists who manage supply chains or programme apps for labour-based platforms such as Uber or Deliveroo can organize marketization via an algorithm. Marketization may not only be brought about by some true believer in the powers of 'the market', but it may also appear as an expedient off-the-shelf solution to policy or business problems, by centre–left governments and corporations barely aware of the intellectual foundations of the techniques they are using. In fact, liberalization, austerity and neoliberal thinking may produce the opposite of marketization if they create noncompetitive markets dominated by monopolies, or if they create markets that fail to deliver on their promises, leading governments to roll back the market (at least those that pay close attention to evaluation studies). The main site of marketization is the business transaction: by changing the processes through which money is exchanged for goods and services, competition can be intensified and pressures on workers ratcheted up.

If marketization sounds technically complex and bureaucratic, that's because it is. This makes it a challenging research topic. There is no global database of all the transactions that may have been recast to promote competition. Instead, we have to find the people who know how prices are formed, how participants are included or excluded, how quality is defined and generally how buyers, sellers and intermediaries interact. And we have to visit them and convince them to educate us on how their market works. In writing this book, we face the challenge of conveying the everyday dramas that play out in the hidden abodes of public-sector procurement, supply-chain management, grant making, the use of market-intermediary apps, and the enforcement of worker rights in workplaces.

Marketization matters in these different contexts, for two main reasons.

First, in capitalist societies, marketization is a tool of class discipline. This means that it changes the power relationship between workers (who have to sell their labour power in exchange for a wage) and capitalists (who can only realize a profit through employing workers). Shifting power relations is sometimes an explicit goal in setting up the market. It can be very effective, when it subjects workers to heightened risks associated with competition, reducing their capacity to demand a better deal from their employers. Capital also faces heightened risks associated with intensified competition, but tends to either reduce them by shaping the rules of the game or insulate itself against them through hedging strategies.

According to some neoclassical economists, more competition should lead to less income inequality because it curbs abuses of private power in markets that lead to extra profits, or 'rents'. This is especially likely when power in a market is concentrated – that is when production or purchasing is dominated by a small number of players, who use their resulting monopsony or monopoly power to shape prices and augment their profits. Consider the case for minimum wage increases made by many US economists. Drawing on Card and Krueger's analysis, the argument is that the laws of supply and demand on the labour market are violated by a small number of fast-food chains that keep wages artificially low by virtue of their domination of demand side (Card and Krueger, 2015). Another way is through corruption or cronyism, whether legal or illegal, which increase private power in markets by subverting market regulation. Fighting monopolies, monosponies, corruption and regulatory capture, seeking transparency, equal treatment and a level competitive playing field – these form the moral case for marketization.

We turn the economists' arguments about competition and equality around. As markets have liberalized in the societies we examine over the past few decades, inequality has increased. How can this be?

In the reality of twenty-first-century Europe, market transactions are being reorganized in ways that protect investors while intensifying price competition. Protecting workers is seldom a major priority, especially at the outset of a marketization process, when the knock-on effects on the institutions of social protection are not part of the discussion. In the worker posting example described earlier, trade unionists could have predicted, based on their knowledge of their industry and the working lives of their members, that creating a single market for construction services across Europe would put downward pressure on wages and working conditions in construction. But efforts to protect construction workers were too little, too late. It took an EU directive and its revision, several CJEU rulings and numerous national reforms to work out how social insurance and industrial relations institutions can co-exist with the freedom of movement of services. The collateral damage of this process included the near-destruction of the German construction union, long spells of unemployment for its members and bankruptcies of many of their employers.

The second main reason why marketization matters is that it tends to insulate decision-making from democratic accountability. Marketization tends to create new mechanisms or institutions, which are shielded from interference from workers or the wider public. Part of the problem is complexity. Markets can be simulated at many levels simultaneously: workplaces, small companies or non-profits or public-sector establishments, large corporations, national governments and the European Union. On a German construction site, German, Polish and Romanian workers will be aware that there is an EU-wide market for construction services. Much more opaque, from their perspective, are the processes through which the prerogatives of the single market are balanced against their own rights at work. They were not afforded much say in deciding whether there should be freedom of movement of services. The treaties, the Commission and the CJEU place limits on the influence workers and their representatives have in these questions. German workers have extensive co-determination rights at the company level and in construction collective agreements extended across the sector by law, but these mean little if their employers are bankrupt and their union crippled. Unions are recognized 'social partners' in the design of some policies within the EU Commission, but they employ far fewer lobbyists than does business. One ideological justification for marketization is transparency, but decision-making in real-world marketization processes is by design opaque to most people affected.

The anti-democratic character of marketization reflects the skepticism of true believers in the market towards popular democracy. Consider not only Hayek's essay on international confederation, but also the support he and his fellow ideologues Milton Friedman and James Buchanan provided for the Chilean dictator Augusto Pinochet, his 1973 coup d'etat, his bloody suppression of socialists, his rollback of social security and public services, and his constitution that locked these policies in for half a century. In their view, and that of many of their fellow neoliberals, economic freedom and political freedom were two different goods, with economic freedom the one to prioritize. As many critical writers on the neoliberal thought collectively have noted, the movement itself was extremely hierarchical, governed in a top–down and secretive manner and dominated by a few wealthy individuals (MacLean, 2017; Mirowski, 2013).

In theory, there are some grounds to be optimistic about the ability of societies to defend themselves from markets. In Polanyian thought, the self-regulated market is always embedded in the social relations from which it sprang and is thought to give rise to a democratic 'counter movement' that reacts against the commodification of land, labour and money. Against the Marxist view of capitalism as deeply disruptive, Polanyians sometimes insist that society will protect itself (Zelizer, 1988).

Yet Europe has experienced a long period of market liberalization and societal disruption without a major democratic countermovement. Social movements in Europe continue to ebb and flow as they always have, and we will show that they sometimes frustrate particular marketization initiatives. A few have been quite effective in intervening in markets by disrupting them (Coderre-LaPalme et al., 2021), introducing social regulations (Jaehrling et al., 2018), organizing the most vulnerable workers (Benassi and Dorigatti, 2015) and in other ways rolling back marketization (Warner and Clifton, 2014). But the last financial crisis was handled in a way that reinforced austerity and very publicly hobbled the democratically elected socialist government in Greece. Brexit has been pursued by a government that, though in many ways illiberal, is unlikely to challenge the prevalence of market competition in British life, and may well seek to extend it further, particularly through punitive measures to push the out-of-work into low-wage jobs (e.g. Butler, 2022). Closer to the ground, where our research takes place, marketization continues.

This book shows why the facts of marketization shouldn't be such a surprise. Marketization can appear as an opaque and bureaucratic concern with process, where the decision-makers involved see themselves as pragmatic problem-solvers and see politics as a hindrance. We will show that marketizers do not always succeed, but when they are tripped up, it is more often due to the realities of everyday life than the kind of protectionist movement that Polanyi detected in nineteenth-century England.

Marketization disciplines workers and subverts democracy. In what follows, we pursue this argument, drawing on many years' worth of interviews with the creators, implementors and victims of marketization across Europe.

2

Capitalist profits and intensified competition

In the second half of the book, we head to the coalface of marketization to examine how it plays out in healthcare, welfare services, and cultural work. Before this, however, we need to look at the issue theoretically. Our introduction raised the broad question of how markets fit into capitalist societies.

This question has been approached from many different angles, some of which we will survey in this chapter. Is the market, as many on the left argue, a totalizing force that subordinates state, society and capital? Or, as many on the centre–left think, can it be tamed or controlled by policymakers, its failures corrected, and society protected? Or maybe, as some libertarians, conservatives and mainstream economists argue, the free market is a real utopia, a path towards spontaneous action of autonomous individuals coordinated to the benefit of overall human welfare in the long run. Although these are not empirical questions – they are about 'the market' in the abstract rather than marketization – any study of the realities of marketization requires us to consider them. In this chapter, we will examine the relationship between capitalists, profits and market competition.

A profit squeeze?

One strange fact about marketization in Europe is that it takes place against the backdrop of capitalist profit-making, in the context of high and increasing inequality. It is puzzling that capitalists would promote marketization, since we might expect an intensified competition between them to squeeze their profits, which should translate into reduced income inequality. Mainstream economists sometimes argue that employers drive down wages through monopsony power in the labour market or drive up prices through monopoly or oligopoly power on markets for goods and services. Economists who disapprove of these violations of market competition call these kinds of profits 'rents' and see government as part of either the problem (especially protectionism, regulatory capture and corruption) or the solution (correcting market failures and reining in private abuses of power in markets). Conventional economic thinking juxtaposes market competition with monopoly and monopsony, with the latter concepts being more often held responsible for increasing inequality and super-profits.

As political economy often points out – be it Marxist, institutional or neoclassical – capitalists and governments frequently do not play by the rules of the free market. When workers combine in unions to fight for improvements in wages and working conditions, as Marx notes in the first volume of *Capital*, a crackdown typically follows, justified by the sacred laws of supply and demand. He also observes that this is hypocrisy: capital itself tends to concentrate and centralize and seek government assistance when necessary, and is not at all heedful of these 'laws' in doing so.

Are supply and demand, the regulators of market competition, laws, or not? In a period of high unemployment, the restructuring of capital puts extra pressure on job seekers who have to compete for a smaller number of jobs, and the resulting pressures may certainly feel like a 'law' from their perspective. However, it is often actually capital which determines both the supply side and demand side of the labour market. Capitalists drive competitors out of business, seeking new forms of labour supply, automating jobs away, changing the labour process and skill requirements, thereby manipulating the demand for labour. In capitalist society, the dice are loaded in favour of capitalists, who in aggregate have considerable influence on the labour market. To some extent they exercise agency over supply and demand, even though the latter sometimes appear to be inviolable 'laws' (Marx, 1976; Chapter 25).

This brings us to the ambivalence of markets. On one hand, markets under capitalism tend to be anarchic, impersonal, and therefore unruly and difficult to bring under control. On the other, they are also governed by rules that have been set by someone. These rules shape how prices are formed and quality measured, who can participate as buyer, seller or intermediary, and how frequent transactions are.

This ambivalence has meant that there are many, sometimes contradictory, ways of thinking about the relationship between capitalists and markets, some of which we will review in this chapter. One thing to consider is that different forms of capital shape markets in different ways. Costas Lapavitsas (2013) shows that in an economy where the main sources of profit come from financial activities (i.e. 'financialization'), the struggles of workers make less of a difference to the functioning of markets than in one dominated by production of commodities. One reason for this is that workers are more organized into unions in industries producing goods than they are in industries overseeing finance and trade. This is because the latter are less labour-intensive and also because more financialized capital tends to be less 'patient' and more aggressive in seeking profit in the short term. Hence, finance capital may enforce and accelerate competitive pressures more potently than industrial capital, a point to which we return in Chapter 3.

Another factor shaping the relationship between capitalists and marketization is the way individual firms organize themselves and their supply chains. The outsourcing trend in car manufacturing was motivated by a desire to reduce costs by purchasing components on the open market – often made by workers with worse pay and working conditions – rather than producing them in-house. But in the 2008–10 crisis some automakers moved to internalize outsourced parts production, because they had underestimated the ability that suppliers had to hold up production (e.g. when workers at axle plants went on strike). In North America, General Motors, Ford and Fiat Chrysler responded by re-purchasing some of the plants that had been spun off and creating more possibilities for trade unionists to negotiate for further insourcing. The costs and benefits of outsourcing are complex and ever-changing, and the assessment of the business case was itself subject to change and re-negotiation (Dupuis and Greer, 2021). Power relations within the corporation can thus lead to certain tasks being removed from the market.

Another example of how power dynamics within supply chains shape the dynamics of competition is provided by the Marxist political economist Ashok Kumar (2020). Kumar examines vast monopsony clothing brands, whose existence in some respects seems a negation of market principles, because they so completely dominate markets (they are the only firms to which small-scale 'sweatshop'-type manufacturer can sell their products). However, they use this monopsony power to engineer intensified competition further down the chain: suppliers must compete fiercely against each other to be able to sell to them. On the other hand, Kumar shows how suppliers can also leverage power of their own by clustering into regional oligopolies. The extent and mechanics of competition are therefore vitally important strategic questions for capital and, as a result, also for labour. Who gets to organize competition, and how?

Moreover, taking part in the exchange process and conducting business transactions involve numerous expenses. Book-keeping, transportation, storage, money, insurance, buying, selling and commercial disputes are all costly activities necessary for the circulation of commodities (Marx, 1978). Marx's controversial discussion of 'unproductive labour' in *Capital* Volumes 2 and 3 is at root a recognition that many of these functions are necessary but don't create any added value. Subsequent economists dubbed these 'transaction costs' and argued that firms will govern transactions with an eye to reducing them (Williamson, 1981). Marx's view was that they tended to increase. Given the amount of detail he provides and the imporance of transaction costs in mainstream economics and management scholarship, it is remarkable how little attention markets and transactions received in subsequent Marxist thought.

In the second half of this book, we will examine in some empirical depth the relationship between capitalists, profits and markets. Mainstream economics assumes that market competition squeezes profits. But capitalists may also wield market forces as a disciplinary weapon within their own spheres of direct influence. Consider three examples. Supply-chain managers at an assembler of cars can use competition between subcontractors to drive down costs. Programmers of an app that connects producers with consumers of a service can write algorithms that stimulate competition with an aim of driving down prices and driving up customer satisfaction. And, as we will show in Chapter 5, even British firms that won government contracts to place unemployed workers in jobs were subcontracting that work to municipalities, charities and other firms, and using aggressive performance management to increase government payments for job outcomes.

In these cases, a dominant market player assumes responsibility for orchestrating competition between other market players on their own terms. Here, the private organizers of the transaction have a powerful sanction to reinforce their control: not renewing the contract with the supplier, excluding the driver from the app or stopping the referral of clients to a subcontractor. Hence, we need to underline an important insight: monopolies and monopsonies are not incompatible with marketization, since a dominant player can impose marketization on its own terms to intensify its own control in markets where they buy or sell. The issue is on whose terms processes of marketization are conducted and who gets to set the rules.

To spell out how capital can benefit from marketization, consider what is common to all three of the examples in the last paragraph: (1) there is a purchaser organized on a large scale that builds uncertainty into the transaction (since the producer may lose the work and even be excluded from the market altogether); (2) the parties to the transaction organize it in a way that is private and sealed off from public oversight, and the purchaser plays a role in setting the rules (deciding what service is to be completed, in what time frame and so on); (3) the players set these rules with an eye to maximizing their own revenues and maintaining or intensifying discipline over those further down the chain. There is no guarantee that capital will succeed in every case, and later we will discuss some cases where it fails. In other cases, as in Kumar's study of global textiles, the power of purchasers may be counteracted by the formation of networks among suppliers. But because marketization processes repeat themselves in many contexts, and capital is more centralized and concentrated than labour, in modern Europe capital has succeeded enough to redistribute wealth, income and power in its favour. That is our theory, at any rate, and in the chapters that follow we discuss varying examples that will allow us to flesh it out.

Alien powers: The agency of capital

We have established that it is important to disentangle the relationship between capitalists, profits and markets. This requires thinking about the *agency* of capitalists. To what extent can they shape market activity in a way that supports their own profit-making? And, to what extent does the market escape this kind of control and exert a disciplinary force of its own?

Capitalist agency, profits and markets

The Austrian Marxist Rudolf Hilferding (1982) provides an influential account of how capitalists come to exercise control over the market, bringing it to heel in an effort to preserve profits. For Hilferding, competition is the 'regulative principle' of capitalist economies. Without competition, capitalist economies lack a motor and don't have reason to produce. But, he proposes, over time, the proportion of investment in fixed capital (i.e. machinery as opposed to workers' wages) tends to increase. As capital is invested in increasingly complex and expensive machinery, and industry becomes more capital-intensive, the time taken to recoup investments increases. This growth in fixed-capital investment leads investors to acquire a longer-term concern for the stability of enterprises. They stand to lose a great deal if those enterprises fail.

The implications of this argument are important for market competition. It suggests that the interests of large-scale investors and managers within firms become bounded together. This is important because these parties might have conflicting material interests and concerns. For instance, a manager might be more preoccupied with skill development and productivity increases, whereas an investor is concerned about the realization of profit. These agendas do not necessarily coincide. But according to Hilferding, as firms become more capital-intensive, both parties develop a shared agenda: the need to preserve the long-term stability of the enterprise and its resistance to short-term market fluctuations, to ensure large-scale capital investments are recouped. The upshot is what Hilferding calls 'finance capital' – the growing importance of very large investors who squeeze out small-scale individual capitalists and have a long-term stake in the managerial oversight of industry.

The next step of Hilferding's story is that finance capital creates its own forms of organization which suppress market competition. The stock exchange, which gives full expression to the short-term fluctuations of the market, is increasingly marginalized. The dominant tendency is for companies to form monopolies and cartels, so that competition in a given industry can effectively be managed and price competition suppressed. This enables profits to be maintained in a context where profits depend increasingly on returns from risky investments in capital-intensive production. The classical Marxist assumption that market competition leads to a tendential decline in the rate of profit is temporarily defeated. But for Hilferding, this is not a sustainable fix for capitalist profitability, because by suppressing the market, finance capital also deprives capitalist economies of their 'regulative principle' which will eventually produce deeper crises.

Hilferding's work was a keystone of much mid-twentieth-century Marxist thought, where it was frequently held that capitalist firms were becoming less influenced by competition and more by corporate organizations. So, particularly post-Second World War, firms would incorporate many different divisions and functions, and allocate resources and tasks between them according to some wider strategic internal plan, rather than sending out different tasks to other companies decided by who offers the best price. The archetypal authority within this kind of vertically integrated firm is not a quick-witted competitor in the marketplace, but the organizational man, who plans and administrates (Baran and Sweezy, 1968). We have already mentioned Kumar's recent work, which provides a more up-to-date insight into the ways capitalists may combine to shift, and potentially suppress, the dynamics of competition to their advantage.

Hilferding's theory is highly relevant here because of the problem it poses: it asks how concretely the actions and agency of capital in the pursuit of profit shape the dynamics of market competition. Although his theory may appear dated in neoliberal Europe, his question is also our question, and his focus on capitalist agency in the pursuit of profits is oddly absent from most accounts of changes in the political economy since the 1970s.

The market as alien power

The dynamics of vertical integration and market suppression identified by Hilferding have been reshaped by changes in international political economy. Financialization has led capitalists to seek profit in financial investments rather than in productive ones (Lapavitsas, 2011). The power of financial markets has for decades now been reflected in the 'shareholder value' ethos (i.e. the promise of short-term returns on financial investments) which has become a more important guiding principle for large firms (Lazonick and O'Sullivan, 2000).

The causes of these political-economic shifts are of less interest here than their consequences for the relationship between capital, profit-making and markets. A more pronounced emphasis on short-term profitability and the growing importance of the 'confidence' of financial investors undermines the more 'patient', production-focused model Hilferding was describing. Market competition once again starts to reassert itself as something to which capitalists have to conform, rather than something they can manage and even suppress.

More recent theorists of neoliberalism have tried to make sense of this apparent resurgence of 'the market'. One way of using this term has been to denote a change in the dominant *rationality* of societies. In other words, how, in general, people in a society think and behave. Inspired by Michel Foucault, some authors chart a supposed shift away from a mentality which accentuates planning and administration, and towards the permeation of a mentality of market competition into every aspect of life. For example, TV shows and books which glorify the 'entrepreneur' and encourage people to believe they can become a successful one may constitute one aspect of this shift. So could many forms of social media, which enable individuals to brand and market themselves as part of a competition for likes and influence. Rather than a citizen who has social rights (for instance to job security, collective bargaining and unemployment insurance), as neoliberal subjects (so the argument goes) we must see ourselves as individual micro-entrepreneurs, ready to invest in our own 'human capital' and act nimbly to improve our situation in competition with others. We have to continually differentiate ourselves, sell our attributes and generally conceive ourselves as a market participant much more deeply than previously. Neoliberalism, in this argument, makes people internalize this rationality (Dardot and Laval, 2010). It achieves this through elaborate systems of quantification and comparison: pay systems in workplaces become more individualized with rewards for the best performers; educational institutions are sorted into complex league tables to decide which is the best 'investment' by students-slash-customers; job seekers are increasingly expected to make themselves into 'employable' individuals by learning 'the rules of the game', so they can out-compete other applicants.

This is a more diffuse analysis than Hilferding's, focused on a wider societal shift in rationality, rather than the mechanics of competition and profit-making. The consequence, in this Foucauldian analysis, is that individuals internalize neoliberal ideas, priming them to take on more risk for themselves, expect less in the way of security and work longer and harder. So, while orthodox Marxists such as Hilferding and Rosa Luxemburg saw expansion (for instance through imperialism) as the main way of boosting profits for capitalists, Foucauldians show how neoliberalism can also boost them through disciplining individuals to work harder and with less complaint, within existing capitalist systems.

This idea of price competition as a disciplinary force which pervades and dominates society is not just a Foucauldian idea. It is also prevalent in more recent Marxist theory. Recent value theory, drawing inspiration from the critical theory of Adorno and Horkheimer, is less focused on class as the central problem in capitalist societies, and more on the totalizing logic of market exchange.[1] Under capitalism, exchange value (the quantitative question of what the commodity can be exchanged for in comparison to other commodities) comes to dominate use value (the actual practical purpose of an object). What should be produced, and how it should be made, is determined exclusively by what can be profitably exchanged in the marketplace.

This has consequences for individuals, because their working life (what they are employed to do and the ways in which they are required to do it) starts to become dominated by this alien force of market exchange: nothing and nobody has value unless it can be measured and compared against other commodities. Their work becomes more tightly controlled and alienating, with individual idiosyncrasies or preferences steamrolled by the abstract 'law of value' (see Wendling, 2009). It also has consequences for societies as a whole. Collectively, we lose the ability to decide which needs are most urgent and how they should be met. Instead, these questions are decided by a swarm of individual organizations all desperately trying to produce things which have exchange value. The dominance of market exchange removes from societies the power to make collective decisions over which commodities to produce, how and to what purpose. This dominance of abstract value over concrete

---

[1]   For a critical overview of these theoretical trends, see Bonefeld (2004) and Cook (2018).

social and individual needs is the central problem of capitalism for value theorists (Hemmens, 2019), more so than the class conflict between workers and capitalists. Value theory sheds light on the way 'the market' comes to dominate society, forming a stark contrast with Hilferding's argument, which sees market competition as being suppressed over time. But this kind of theorizing, like with the Foucauldian literature about neoliberal subjectivity, neglects two other aspects of our inquiry, about which Hilferding had much to say: profits and capitalists (that is to say, capitalists as individuals or organizations with agency to shape the world, rather than as mere pawns of abstract value).

For value theorists, the downgrading of these factors is sometimes part of the point. Debates in and around Britain's Labour Party provide an example of this. Pitts and Bolton (2018) use value theory explicitly to dismiss arguments which frame capital and capitalists as a potentially malign agency in society (as when the former Labour leader Jeremy Corbyn referred to a 'rigged system'). To do so, they argue, is to miss just how abstract and impersonal the forces shaping our societies actually are. They go further, claiming that, once someone does start pointing towards particular groups or organizations as a cause of inequality or exploitation, this opens the door to all sorts of problems: nationalism (the problems are the fault of another country or national group), conspiracy theory (the fault of shadowy plotters), populism (the fault of arrogant elites) or anti-Semitism (the fault of a conspiracy by Jewish people). In fact, according to their reading of value theory, the problem is not that individuals 'rig' capitalist economies. The whole system of market exchange and value extraction, they argue, actually dominates more or less everyone within it, including capitalists.

These branches of theory (Foucauldian literature and neo-Marxian writing on value) have the benefit of highlighting the idea of *market discipline* as a means of supporting profit-making. This is an important part of our theory, but it has important limitations. Value theory typically presents the exchange process as a domineering force at a very high level of abstraction. The 'law of value' therefore becomes such an all-encompassing power that it emerges as a kind of Rorschach test which value theorists use to justify very different conclusions. For Alastair Hemmens, an advocate of value theory who has written extensively about the history of French thought on the subject, realizing the totalitarian nature of the law of value means we need to focus on constructing a different way of life, where the market is put back in its place. But for Pitts and Bolton, the response should be a 'pessimistic liberalism'. In their view, the dangers of an excessively 'personalized' analysis (as manifested in political rhetoric from Donald Trump's anti-China monologues to Jeremy Corbyn's invocation of the 'rigged system') are worse than the dominance of capitalist exchange itself. Hence, the best option is to embrace impersonal liberal institutions which protect individuals against the ravages of populism and conspiracy theory. The law of value prevents us from doing anything more ambitious.

Although this approach highlights the discipline of the market in the abstract, it neglects important layers of empirical reality. At a lower level of abstraction, we find many institutions with real, material effects on the way competition is organized, which we will examine throughout this book. It is impossible to understand these empirical phenomena without paying some attention to the agency of particular groups or organizations. An undue focus on abstract market forces (and dismissal of any analyses which present capitalism as in some way 'rigged') ignores the interests and concrete mechanisms which shape the development and application of market mechanisms. It is the latter that is our focus here. To understand this, we are led back towards Hilferding and his interest in the agency of capitalists, but with the difference that we observe capitalists using their agency to intensify price competition, rather than suppressing it.

The management of transactions

What, then, are the specific features of transactions that are so useful for exerting class discipline? Economists examining make-or-buy decisions (i.e. whether to outsource or keep functions in-house) often argue that transactions are governed in a way that minimizes transaction costs, and that this depends on the nature of the good or service being produced (Williamson, 1981). Some goods and services may be more conducive to being outsourced (cleaning, catering and call centres) than others (senior management), but even for these examples there are important caveats and exceptions.

In our later chapters, we will show that it's not simply that the nature of the good or service defines the way the transaction is organized (for instance, whether a service is outsourced or executed in-house). The reverse may often be true: transactions are frequently governed with an eye to re-engineering the service being exchanged. For instance, a government might pay a private company to 'support' job seekers, while building incentives into the contract that tie payment to the number of people pushed into work. In this case, the terms of the transaction shape the way the service will be delivered, not vice versa. Hence, the features of the service being bought and sold are the effect, not cause, of the way the transaction is governed. As Marx argues in *Capital* Volume 2, the costs of business transactions tend to increase with capitalist growth. Transactions, therefore, matter for capital, not mainly from the perspective of efficiency, but also because they are powerful tools of coordination and control.

In the introduction we argued that marketization as a real-world process has three dimensions: facilitating market entry, increasing the frequency of transactions and improving comparability between goods and services. We will now elaborate on each of these points in turn.

Facilitating market entry

For markets to be competitive, they have to be open to new participants and participants have to have some reason to participate. Opening up national markets to international competition is at the root of the European integration project and the main reason why the freedom of movement of goods, services, capital and labour has been so transformative. Opening markets can take place domestically as well, as when a health service or public employment service creates opportunities for for-profit companies to bid to deliver services. Encouraging marginalized people to look for paid work or making it possible for them to access customers directly through an app are two ways to facilitate the entry of workers into the labour market.

When openings are created, however, it is not automatic that new participants will enter. Our empirical chapters will reveal variants on this problem, but it is one that the managers of transactions have to contend with. Participants can be attracted to the market through inducements, such as attractive wages, prices or subsidies. In Britain, minimum wage increases during the New Labour era were motivated in part by their incentive effects in coaxing potential workers into the labour market. Wage subsidies are another common tool for governments to encourage employers to hire job seekers. Similarly, governments creating public-service markets have numerous tools at their disposal to encourage participation, even if these might entail less competition along other dimensions – for instance long contracts or generous prices. In some cases, the marketizer simply creates competitors, as the British government did when it created Working Links, its joint venture with the private sector that until its 2019 bankruptcy was a major player in Britain's employment services market. The business of luring, accommodating or even creating market participants is an important, often expensive and complicated, aspect of marketization.

Participants may also be 'attracted' to markets because the alternative is worse. The prospect of starvation was a centrally important work incentive in Marx's discussion of worker-to-worker competition and the industrial reserve army in *Capital* Volume 1. By reducing the generosity of jobless benefits, increasing conditions and sanctions and generally making life more miserable for job seekers, policymakers reinstate the discipline of the market for large numbers of workers at the bottom of the labour market. If it is not already true that any job is better than no job, policymakers can add punishments, take away benefits, and make it true.

Policymakers and capitalists thus take quite concrete steps to open markets and encourage new players to participate, not just by removing restrictions but also through rewards (mainly for investors) and punishments (mainly for workers).

Making transactions more frequent

For markets to be competitive, transactions have to be repeated. Otherwise, when one person or organization wins some business, they keep it, and competition dissipates. Take live music work as an example to illustrate this point. As we will show in Chapter 6, freelance musicians living from one-off gigs have to constantly compete to access new work. This is not the case for tenured symphony orchestra musicians, who may keep their position for many years after a successful initial audition. Similarly, the manager of a training company financing her organization by collecting tuition fees or state-issued vouchers must constantly compete for learners; this is not true for a state school funded to provide education for all pupils in a certain catchment area. Marketizers in education dream of abolishing tenure for teachers and issuing vouchers to parents, because both lead to more frequent transactions, disciplining educators through continuous competition.

One common way to increase the frequency of transactions is to reduce the length of contracts. Imagine that a provider of social services stops receiving ongoing grant support from a government funder, but instead is switched to one-year contracts. The potential points of contact where the internal life of the organization meets the open market are multiplied, and this constrains what management does in many ways (Marchington et al., 2005). Market discipline becomes much tighter, since if the provider does not satisfy its client, it could lose its funding in a matter of months. Any worker voice within the firm is likely to be displaced by the influence of the funder, and managers may shift risk onto workers through short-term employment contracts mirroring the timing of their contracts with government. Workers and managers will have to justify their own existence each time they re-apply for funding, and in a competitive market this will mean being benchmarked against others in terms of their cost and performance each time. At some point, managers will fail to renew the organization's funding, because the contract is won by one of their competitors, and staff either become unemployed, are redeployed internally, or transfer to the new organization. In a country like Germany, while workers have strong rights to participate in decisions within workplaces, there is little statutory basis for worker representatives to influence these interactions between organizations (Doellgast and Greer, 2007). A whole realm of political-economic activity, with vital implications for working conditions, is shut off from worker influence.

Now consider: the manager within the service provider reports to the funder how difficult planning has become, how staff have become demoralized and how much additional effort has to go into replacing staff and bidding for new work. The funder then agrees to shift the work into a two-year contract, with an option for a one-year extension. This may not please some of this provider's competitors, and it does make it difficult for the funder to redeploy resources in future years if there is a sudden change in needs. However, with a longer contract, planning the internal operations of the service provider becomes more realistic. Because the market discipline on the firm is reduced, the class discipline within the firm may also be. Workers' positions are more secure, which may mean they have more capacity to influence the nature of their jobs and the terms under which they are conducted. As we will show later, this may also improve the quality of the services and reduce the amount the funder spends on competitive tendering exercises.

These are not hypothetical examples but reflect real pressures that organizations we visited were under when contracting with public authorities, as well as the dilemmas that the public authorities faced in dealing with their contractors. We will explore them in detail in later chapters. Increasing the frequency of transactions was an important feature of all of our cases. In music, we saw how digitalized agencies were shifting to a higher-volume model. Rather than setting up ongoing relationships with particular buyers (like a hotel chain or events company, as a traditional live music agent might do), they required musicians to compete again and again for a stream of smaller one-off gigs. They demanded that this process proceeds quickly, and this emphasis on speed and volume not only intensified the pressure for musicians to reduce their prices but also stripped away their ability to negotiate with potential clients.

Increasing the frequency of transactions is a way to ramp up discipline on market participants that disproportionately affects workers. Firms often adapt by shifting the risks onto workers through short-term contracts or the use of freelancers. Workers have far fewer options in hedging these risks, and the case of front-line workers in marketized employment services becomes similar to that of musicians: alternating periods of work and unemployment, with an ongoing need to compete for work, income and ultimately survival.

Comparability and commodification

If they are to be subjected to market competition, even services like health and social care must be recast as commodities. This requires changes to the price mechanism to more clearly specify how prices relate to the good or service being offered. An organization funded by ongoing grants for the purpose of serving marginalized young people will have a much less commodified service than one with a contract to deliver an introductory German-language course for a year. In the former case, government might pay social workers to carry out a function that the workers themselves define in line with their occupational ethos, and which involves a large number of qualitative professional judgements which are tailored to the situation. In the latter case, it is the government funder that defines the service or outcome that is being purchased. In the latter case the nature of the service is defined, in a more transparent way, by the organizer of the transaction.

In public services, specifying the service is arguably a common-sense method for making the process transparent, but many of our interviewees pointed out that attempting to define and measure 'quality' for these services is often anything but straightforward. This was subject to intense debate in Brussels during the time we were doing our research: when are government-funded health and social service subject to competition law, and if they are not subject to competition law, then how can governments be held accountable for their decisions? The concern among many officials in the EU Commission was that officials in many member states were responding to political pressures or rewarding their cronies, instead of purchasing the lowest-cost, highest-quality provider of services through procedures that assured equal treatment and transparency.

At the time of writing, in the UK, one of the most prominent criticisms levelled at the Conservative government's handling of the NHS during the pandemic has been along similar lines. The former Health Secretary Matt Hancock was accused by political opponents of giving lucrative contracts to favoured contacts, rather than going through a fair tendering procedure.[2] At issue was whether discussions about public-funded services should be subject to the market-making principles that the EU Commission was enforcing in other areas of life. The Commission does not necessarily demand privatization, or even competitive tendering, for publicly funded services; but officials take very seriously principles of transparency and equal treatment.

In Brussels, we also met trade unionists and lobbyists with a background in health and social services who were worried by the pressures to prescribe services in detail and to use price-based competitive tendering. One problem was that this threatened to make skilled professionals subordinate to a government purchasing agent, which could negatively affect the quality of services. Because the information they collect and act on in their everyday work is simply not available to the public officials who would define the work, front-line professionals need discretion and flexibility to do their jobs (Lipsky,

---

[2] For typical news coverage, see Crichton (2021). In the article, a Labour MP alleges: 'you were more likely to get a contract for PPE in the NHS if you knew Matthew Hancock rather whether or not you could actually supply and were an expert in it.'

1980). Certainly, prescribing the work in detail to facilitate purchasing in compliance with procurement law was not conducive to innovation from front-line workers. With much justification (as discussed in Chapter 4), critics of marketization argue that a disciplined workforce stripped of autonomy and discretion would not produce the highest-quality social services. In our data, as the service became more like a standardized commodity, innovation in response to changing local needs and labour markets became more difficult.

Another problem with defining the service in this way is that many questions about the use of resources are removed from the realm both of worker voice and public deliberation. What kinds of service are needed, what counts as high quality, is it acceptable to de-fund existing services, and what role should price play in selecting the service? If market-makers succeed in turning services into something that is readily bought and sold, and where quality is defined by 'transparent' criteria set by purchasing offices, these questions are handled in a way that is deliberately insulated from politics. Standardized pricing of diagnoses, competitive tendering, vouchers or other methods to re-cast services as commodities: all of these are devised with little or no input from workers or the public.

Defining a service as a commodity, with clearly quantifiable characteristics that enable price comparisons, is an important precondition of marketization. In later chapters, we will show how a wide variety of market mechanisms facilitate downward pressure on costs or prices and restrict the agency of workers delivering services. In other words, they act as a force for class discipline.

Inequality and class discipline

Marketization affects workers differently from capitalists. The constraints imposed by intensified price competition tend to devalue work and deskill jobs; they have undermined job security as well as the institutions that protect workers and give them voice. While marketization has had these disciplinary effects on workers, capital finds new profit-making opportunities and new forms of regulation sealed off from 'politics'. The effects of marketization, as it exists in empirical reality, are thus class-biased.

This argument is at odds with much economic thought. Whether it is a telecommunications oligopoly gouging customers or fast-food employers using their monopsony power to squeeze worker wages, mainstream economics sees anti-competitive behaviour as an important cause of inequality. Hilferding's example of German capitalists in the late nineteenth century using cartels to increase the rate of profit has a similar lesson. Whether mainstream or heterodox, much political economy suggests that competition squeezes profits and places checks on the market power of capitalists and that capitalists rebel against the laws of supply and demand and resist the discipline of the market.

However, monopolies and intensified competition are not mutually exclusive, since the capitalists that dominate one market can simultaneously organize competition in another. In our early research, we became interested in the supply-chain management of auto assemblers like Volkswagen, which stimulated competition to cut costs in their supply chain, even creating new firms to compete and telling suppliers producing in Germany to reduce their costs by moving to low-wage countries (Greer, 2008). In other markets, like Britain's employment services, described further, the state hands over the capacity to organize markets to large firms. This case is instructive, because the government chose transactions that were infrequent (due to long contracts) deliberately to give companies the ability to plan their services and realize a return on investment. Meanwhile, these large firms shifted risks onto their workforce and their subcontractors through aggressive performance management. In this marketization case, competition is suppressed in one area (the for-profit main contractors) and intensified in another (the local authorities, charities and smaller firms that worked as their subcontractors).

Another example of this tendency is the online platform, a firm that is also an open market. For true believers in 'the market' the concept is intriguing: a monopolist or oligopolist that uses an app to organize competitive exchanges between producers and consumers, using algorithms and big data to coordinate vast amounts of economic activity, sidestepping some of the problems with bureaucratic central planning (Moazed and Johnson, 2016). In Chapter 6, we will discuss the platform economy in live music, a sector which was relatively weakly platformized, with no player achieving concentrated monopoly power, though not for want of trying. There are many live music platforms and digitalized intermediaries to choose from (not just for clients, but musicians themselves can create profiles in multiple places). But for working musicians in niches where these sites have established themselves, that makes little difference.

Each platform or digitalized agency can stage intense market competition, whether monopolists or not, because they have managed to position themselves in such a way that they orchestrate the exchange process. For the musicians, what matters is the micro-market engineered by the individual agency they are dealing with, which sets the parameters for intense competition between acts on the roster. Attaining a monopoly would make profit-making easier for a given agency, but even without that they extract profits and affect the working lives of musicians through their role as market organizers.

Private capitalists may derive power through their own positions as monopolists or monopsonists, but if they organize market competition then they are also vectors for marketization. In doing so, they concentrate their class power in a way that gives them the ability to wield disciplinary force over workers and other market participants. The second half of this book will contain many similar examples of class discipline imposed via price-based competition.

Governments organizing markets have to deal with the question of how investors can achieve returns (since if returns appear unlikely, they may struggle to generate market participants). This is not straightforward given the multiple policy goals, the complex legacy of public bureaucracy, and potential political embarrassment when marketization leads to high cost or low quality. The long contracts and the discretion given to service providers on Britain's Work Program is one example of governments responding directly to the concerns of the financial sector to incentivize private investment. We will discuss it in Chapter 4. However, in the world of employment services, this approach is unique. For-profit companies have struggled in the German and French markets due to the power of the state and local networks, respectively, in setting the rules of the market. The question of incentivizing investment is also present in debates over healthcare marketization. Reducing the competitive advantages of the public sector vis-a-vis the private sector is an explicit goal of various different mechanisms which we will examine in Chapter 5.

The question of who to reward has a flip side: who to discipline. While there may be mechanisms to hold private firms accountable in public markets, the disciplinary power of the state is much greater on the working class. Punitive active labour-market schemes are an obvious instrument for disciplining workers. Through a mix of punishments and supports they force jobless people who otherwise could subsist outside the market into low-wage and precarious work. Even if only a small number of employers recruit through their programmes, by increasing the misery of job seekers while also giving them a clear path into the bottom of the labour market, supply and demand are rigged in capital's favour. This was not only a problem for job seekers: as we will see, workers with jobs also found themselves subject to increasingly tight performance management, both in employment services and healthcare.

The discipline of the market extends beyond the working class to the democratic polity as a whole, and its consequences extend beyond the distribution of income to the distribution of power. Health and welfare services demand democratic accountability, which could be imposed not only through direct control over services by democratically elected politicians (as in many public services) but also through giving representatives of workers and service users positions in the boards that govern these services. Democratic accountability, however, tends to obstruct marketization, as we will explain in later chapters.

How, then, can marketization be used to redistribute power? Marketization requires a set of rules, defined from the centre and which tend to squeeze out the more deliberative or qualitative considerations that wider democratic participation requires. Major decisions in marketized systems tend to be conducted in circumstances insulated from democratic scrutiny. This is as true for the business of setting the rules of the competitive game in its supply chain as it is for politically sensitive decisions such as the selection of contractors under those rules. We now, therefore, turn to the role of the state.

3

Marketization, the state and class discipline

The previous chapter discussed how capitalists may initiate or manipulate marketization, but in our data the key marketizer is often the state itself. As we move to examine marketization in practice in the second half of the book, we will see that the role of the state becomes a puzzle. Our research will show how marketization, especially in public services, is expensive and laborious to implement. It raises numerous problems, some unforeseen and some predictable. It frequently faces resistance from many different quarters and often performs disappointingly even when judged on its own terms. Indeed it is often so difficult, it hardly seems worth the trouble. Yet governments, as we show in the next two chapters, have continued with successive waves of market reforms to health and welfare systems. Why?

First, we must consider the context of capitalist societies, in which all of our observations take place. One defining feature of them is the class relationship between labour and capital. A 'capitalist' is an individual or organization who makes an investment – for example in the production of a good or service – with the expectation of realizing a profit from it. 'Labour' refers to the workers who produce these goods and services, and hence whose efforts make profit possible. The relationship between labour and capital is complicated, because it involves both cooperation and conflict. Without some degree of cooperation nothing can get done. But there is also a deep-lying conflict of interest, since capitalists need to extract more profit in exchange for less outlay, while workers have an interest in increasing their wage relative to the labour they put in. The ambivalence of the labour–capital relationship is a source of unpredictability and instability, and it is often hard to predict where conflict will emerge, and how. Sometimes, workers may surprisingly accept conditions that appear detrimental and in other circumstances they may fiercely contest them. This is complicated further by various other factors which mediate the labour–capital relationship, most importantly the state.

The relationship between labour and capital is underpinned by the process of capital accumulation. Capitalist economies undergo a perpetual cycle where surpluses are constantly being extracted and either reinvested on an expanded scale or skimmed off and distributed to investors. This process of extracting and reinvesting profits and accumulating capital cannot stop. If it does, the economy stalls. So, even if capitalist accumulation produces some profound dysfunctions (not just in the relationship between labour and capital but also, for instance, climate change or structural racism), under the logic of capitalist economies the process of profit extraction and reinvestment needs to continue. State intervention is often required to make this possible. This could be in the form of corporate bailouts after financial crises; of furlough schemes to prevent the economy imploding in a pandemic; or of placing restrictions on strikes if workers' movements appear a threat to capitalist stability.

Marketization therefore needs to be understood by looking at the power relationships between labour and capital. Both groups have weapons at their disposal to strengthen their position relative to the other. Understanding these quickly brings us to the role of the state. Workers may band together to extract improvements in living and working conditions from employers and governments. Sometimes they win achievements such as new legal rights and protections (for instance, limits on the working day or better social protections against unemployment). Employers may also turn to the state to enforce order in the workplace and labour market (for instance in restrictions on what trade unions are allowed to do, or in a liberalization of laws governing hiring and firing). We will show that marketization, as it has played out in twenty-first-century Europe, has rejigged these power relationships in favour of capital.

We will show how the concept of class discipline helps to explain the attraction of marketization for governments. We have defined class discipline as any process which increases capitalists' ability to reshape working conditions as they see fit, and reduces workers' ability to influence this process. While most discussions of inequality use statistical figures like the Gini coefficient, ours is qualitative: we have in mind it is the shifting power imbalance at work that we have in mind. Hence, various different processes could be broadly described as some form of class discipline. Legislation which restricts strike activity is an obvious example. Rolling back the welfare state might have class disciplinary effects since it makes workers more scared of unemployment and hence more accepting of low-paid and insecure work. When a firm deskills workers (for instance by finding a way of replacing a process which required rare, and hence expensive, skills with a simpler one that could be done by anyone), this might also have class disciplinary effect because workers' bargaining power declines with the demand for their unique skills. Marketization, too, in the context of twenty-first-century European political economy, is very often about class discipline.

We have already noted that marketization takes diverse forms – from ratcheting up competitive pressures in the delivery of public services to the creation of platforms and increasingly competitive supply-chain management practices for the private sector. It is enacted by many different people with different goals. In the second half of the book, we show that the competitive landscape is heterogeneous, with important sector and country variations. Our argument is not that every instance of marketization is class discipline, and we are not trying to tell a master narrative of contemporary life that contains all the causes and consequences of what we see. But we will argue that the curious international persistence of marketization in modern Europe is impossible to explain without some reference to class discipline.

When we look at marketization in health, welfare and music, we will find that certain features turn up repeatedly. In each of these cases, marketization tends to disempower workers and threaten their pay and security, undermine job roles and professional statuses which hinder profit extraction, and weaken institutions that might help workers get a better deal. Meanwhile, they tend to confer to capitalists the power to organize transactions on their terms, thus insulating profits against the consequences of intensified competition and also from democratic accountability.

Marketization is contested, however. The following chapters provide numerous examples of workers and citizens fighting back against it. For this reason, we will also discuss the politics of marketization. We have already argued that marketization has an uncomfortable relationship with 'politics'. The pioneers of neoliberal thought believed that it was important to insulate markets from politics, and later we will illustrate how the institutions and tools of marketization are often designed to obscure political interference or oversight. Pepper Culpepper's (2010) distinction between 'quiet' and 'noisy' politics is useful here. Noisy politics are the politics of protest and popular dispute. They affect areas of policymaking that attract the interest of journalists (like, for instance, the privatization of a major public hospital). This is what advocates of marketization we interviewed meant when they bemoaned the frustrating role of 'politics'. Quiet politics is different: it is the business of setting and implementing rules that do not attract the attention of journalists and do not attract protest. Culpepper notes that, with quiet politics, business interests tend to get their way due to their inherent privileges as business elites and due in part to their superior lobbying firepower. Their success in policymaking is less certain where noisy politics are involved. We will find marketization tending to not only progress through quiet politics and stumbling when encountering noise but will also show how resistance to marketization can be quiet.

Class discipline, we argue, is not a regrettable side effect of marketization policies which are otherwise necessary to obtain low-cost high-quality goods and services. Class discipline is in many cases an end in itself, even if it's very rarely put in these terms by the people doing it. It is given euphemisms, such as instilling a 'work ethic' among job seekers, breaking the power of unions representing front-line workers to 'obstruct' desired reforms or making non-profit or public-sector social service workers more 'accountable'. In the context of a heavily financialized and opaque global economic order, class disciplinary measures are an important method of boosting 'business confidence', no matter if they are counterproductive, even disastrous, in other ways. This is the argument we will explore throughout this chapter.

Stable policy systems and external shocks

Explaining marketization takes us into the terrain of political science, because it requires us to grapple with questions of why governments make the kinds of policies they do. Government policy matters for marketization, whether the market is directly made by government or the government merely creates a framework that allows private actors to organize competition. Why do such public policies seem to vary so much across different countries? And, why do particular national ways of making policy seem to persist?

Public policies emanate primarily from government institutions and the formally constituted organizations such as unions and business associations that can influence them. However, many other factors also exert an influence on policy, including less tangible forces like cultural or political norms and dominant ideas. The ensemble of all of these things, formal and informal, can be called a 'policy system'. Policy systems are known for their 'stickiness'; the self-reinforcing logic that makes change difficult and renders them quite conservative (Pierson, 2000). A given country will have a particular policy system that tends to shape how things are done and rule out options which deviate too far from this. The parties that lead governments may change but without altering the frameworks guiding how they can act when in power.

According to this approach, change is therefore usually gradual but may accelerate under conditions of a shock. A global financial crisis may force a rethink of some economic policies (Campbell and Pedersen,

2014), and the same may happen during a pandemic. When a crisis happens, the dominant ideas informing policy may change, influenced also by the actions of various think tanks and policy entrepreneurs, and often the deliberate marginalization of actors that may be wedded to the previous status quo and hence resist change (Morgan and Hauptmeier, 2021). But even under these circumstances, governments can never rework policy systems using a blank slate. Policy does not change through a Darwinian process in which failed ideas are discarded and replaced with ideas better adapted to the environment. Governments respond even to major external shocks by drawing on the same ideas and material interests and through the same institutional mechanisms that existed before the shock (Hall, 2018). Policies may be 'locked in' when, despite evidence mounting to show that they don't work very well, they don't go away. Policy systems, from this perspective, are thus path-dependent (Hassink, 2005).

A particularly influential version of this type of argument is Varieties of Capitalism (VOC), which divides the world's rich capitalist countries into two camps (Hall and Soskice, 2001). Liberal Market Economies (LMEs), which normally includes a group of countries with Anglophone dominant cultures (normally the United Kingdom and United States but sometimes Canada, the Antipodes and Ireland) in contrast with Coordinated Market Economies (CMEs) which includes various other countries (often Germany and the Nordic countries, Japan and some other Continental European countries such as the Netherlands). The institutions of LMEs favour markets as the main method of coordination, whether through weak worker participation rights in the firm, restricted and stingy welfare provision, arms-length contracting relations and low collective bargaining coverage. CMEs, by contrast, rely on non-market coordination of business, including stronger worker participation, more generous social insurance, strong relations in the business community and widespread collective bargaining.

In VOC theory, different institutional systems are supposed to be mutually reinforcing, because they provide a basis for strong capitalist growth. A CME should have a comparative advantage in manufacturing cars and machine tools, because its institutions produce and protect the skills and knowledge for the kind of incremental innovation needed, and because of partnerships between banks, lead firms and suppliers that have a similar effect. The British government, by contrast, is unlikely to adopt similar institutions. Why? Because it doesn't fit with the strategies of businesses in sectors such as finance and biotech that allegedly benefit from Britain's liberal market institutions, since they are supposedly focused on rapid and radical types of innovation in response to market shifts.

VOC theory would lead us to expect marketization to be mainly confined to LMEs, except as a marginal phenomenon. Trying to impose marketization on CMEs, according to VOC, is supposed to be like fitting a square peg into a round hole. But this book will show examples of profound marketization in CMEs, including Germany, Finland and France, in which governments have gone to great lengths to make the round hole square. The cases of marketization we have looked at are by no means limited to LMEs like the UK.

The idea of policy lock-in might chime nicely with the way we have described marketization. Indeed, we will show that marketization policies have negative effects, but continue nonetheless. Is marketization therefore just a locked-in effect of sticky policy systems? This is also not the case. Marketization cannot be described as a locked-in policy. Quite the reverse. It is often a radically disruptive force, which rearranges and disorganizes existing patterns of behaviour. Marketization may seem a conservative policy in some respects, because it tends to reinforce hierarchies and undermine the capacity of workers to challenge elites. But it is often a dramatic departure from existing policy arrangements, which cannot be anticipated by looking at the history of countries' policy systems.

Certainly, looking at differences across national policy systems might help explain the *manner* in which marketization has happened. It's plausible, for instance, that the particular forms taken by marketization in healthcare to some extent reflect path-dependent national differences. In Chapter 4, for instance, we will examine how the British state's go-to marketization techniques reflect a long history of reliance on corporate contacts to accomplish challenging tasks. Meanwhile, in France, marketization has been pushed through much more direct and hands-on state orchestration. But it is important not to miss the forest for the trees. The variations in the form marketization takes – the market mechanisms – are the trees. The forest is marketization itself, which in some form or another, is found in all these contexts. Theories about path-dependent policy systems don't help to explain this.

Another way of explaining marketization might be to look at the way particular ideas spread from country to country. Much research looks at the transnational diffusion of neoliberalism since the 1970s. This term, as we saw, roughly denotes not only a shift towards greater emphasis on the market as a policy tool but also the 'rationality' shaping individuals' everyday lives (Lane, 2011). Think tanks have played a crucial role in disseminating neoliberal thinking internationally (Mirowski and Plehwe, 2015). Is marketization explained by the growing international permeation of neoliberal ideas?

Proponents of this perspective also emphasize the importance of shocks. The economic crises of the 1970s, in this version of events, led to a discrediting of Keynesian theory which had been highly influential since the Second World War. This failure boosted 'the persuasive power of the market' (Peters et al., 2005), and previously powerful actors such as trade unions lost their influence in policy debates (Mudge, 2008). This means there was (a) a desire for radical thinking and (b) a lack of influential voices to oppose neoliberal initiatives. Add to this the increasing effectiveness of business lobby groups internationally, and there is a strong possible explanation for why neoliberalism has spread across many countries, hence marketization.

But the puzzle is still not solved. In fact, this raises a deeper question. Do crises really discredit old models and create space for new ideas? If so, why did the global financial crisis of 2008 lead to so few fundamental changes? The US government's economic response to the 2020 Covid-19 crisis was modelled on its approach to the 2008 financial crisis (Brenner, 2020). Our chapters on health and welfare show that marketization has not in general been rolled back since 2008. Despite the intellectual crisis of neoliberalism, its diminished legitimacy and concrete setbacks faced by marketizers, policymakers continue to use market mechanisms. Marketization is not a conservative overhang of old policy ideas, nor is it a pragmatic change of tack in response to crisis. So what is it?

When states disrupt themselves

Consider the example with which we started this book. The Hartz IV reforms, the wave of privatizations and the decline of collective bargaining in Germany were a sharp break with aspects of the established national model. They were not explicable in terms of Germany's existing policy systems. German state and German industry create new mechanisms to engineer shifts away from existing welfare and collective bargaining arrangements. They did not shy away from marginalizing the established 'social partners', weakening their institutional bases in the Ministry of Labor and public employment service. This was an important way that they sought a shift towards neoliberal ideas (Morgan and Hauptmeier, 2021), with concrete material consequences.

Compare this to marketizing reforms in employment services, which we will examine in Chapter 4. In Germany after the Hartz reforms, the public employment service created a powerful purchasing function to ensure transparency, equal treatment and competition on the basis of price and quality of services. This put strains on the long-established tissue of local non-profits providing employment services to vulnerable people. In France, by contrast, when policymakers attempted to overwrite their system with a new model, in which for-profit providers played a pre-eminent role, they were not so successful. They created new contracting arrangements to attract multinational for-profit service providers, made substantial changes to targets and incentive systems, and introduced new procedures for orchestrating competition between potential providers. In Seine-Saint-Denis, where we did our research, this hadn't worked, because the grafting of the marketized system on top of the existing one had been too awkward and unwieldy, and the institutions of the French state had been unable to successfully dislodge the latter. And, as we will demonstrate, the disconnect between the benefits system and employment services meant that the state lacked a vital coercive lever with which to impose a cohesive marketized model. Contrast this again with Germany and the UK, where the threat of benefits sanctions have been used to force 'customers' to play along with the rules of marketized workfare.

We will also look at Slovenia, where a similar dynamic played out as in France, this time with less impediment. Here, marketizing reforms were pushed more strongly from the EU level. Marketization was more disruptive than it was in France, and the established network of local non-profit organizations providing employment services was genuinely thrown into disarray. This more chaotic situation was ushered in where the state developed a new infrastructure for competitive tendering, but struggled to find credible providers. We will show how job security, professional status and reliable career pathways for the front-line workers delivering these services had deteriorated as a result.

We will revisit these cases in later chapters, because they show how heterogeneous the specific mechanisms that impose marketization can be in different contexts and how much outcomes can vary. For now, we just need to note that, throughout our empirical story, marketization will certainly not come across as a pragmatic response to crisis or as emanating from the logic of existing policy systems. Which government is more pragmatic: the one that is willing to pay the price of creating and sustaining a market or the one that abandons marketization after an unsuccessful experiment? In our case studies, marketization sometimes produced ruptures and were often in conflict with relatively settled existing arrangements. The latter generated obstacles to marketization initiatives – noisy campaigns and bureaucratic resistance – that states had to overcome in order to stimulate competition.

This is especially clear when looking at healthcare systems, as we will do in Chapter 5. Consider marketizing reforms in the English NHS.

They have been painstaking and expensive. They have involved the creation of new institutions from scratch, as well as the development of detailed new rules and procedures for commissioning. Our research will reveal how much time and resources this had consumed, as well as the generally negative effects they had on quality. There was often resistance at local level, for these very reasons, not just from trade unions and public campaigners but also from public servants within the system who complied in a reluctant or foot-dragging manner. Once again, our account of marketization reveals a story of intense centrally driven disruption.

French healthcare is different from the NHS but here, again, the central state was architect of a difficult and conflictual process of marketization. The mechanisms used to intensify price competition were different. Financialization of infrastructure through Public Finance Initiatives (PFIs), for instance, was widespread in the NHS but much less of a feature in France. Instead, the main driving force behind marketization was change to the funding of health services, specifically the introduction of fixed-price reimbursement rates (where all procedures are assigned their own monetary costs by government, which then reimburses hospitals according to the procedures they have completed). We will show how these were widely perceived to create new dysfunctions, particularly through their threat to the way healthcare was delivered by front-line workers. Institutionally, the French system also became messier. New regional institutions had been developed supposedly to increase the health system's responsiveness to local needs. But the policy tools at their disposal were being stripped away by the new funding system, which privileged the centrally imposed framework for orchestrating competition above local autonomy. Where local authorities sought to reshape systems more informally according to their own priorities, this tended to precipitate new waves of central direction (see Guerrero et al., 2009). During the pandemic, the Macron government came under pressure to revise the hospital funding system, but his cabinet remains attached to its principles (Sicot, 2020).

The role of the state in engineering marketization is also clear when examining labour-market regulation across developed capitalist countries. Baccaro and Howell (2011) chart the development of labour-market institutions in fifteen countries from 1974 to 2005. They show that institutions, such as collective bargaining, have not disappeared, but have been reformed in different ways in different countries. Some have shifted collective bargaining to the workplace level or abolished it, while others have moved to coordinate bargaining across the entire economy. The *outcome* of these changes, however, has been the same. In all cases, workers' voice in collective bargaining was weakened and impediments to capitalists making quick decisions over workforce issues such as pay and job security were reduced. The clear aim is to make it easier for private-sector actors to respond to market signals, without being hindered by social regulations in whatever form. As Howell (2016) has argued elsewhere, governments have been extremely important in directing this process. Initiatives to make collective bargaining systems more capital-friendly often run up against the 'stickiness' of existing institutions and the residual power of organizations like trade unions. It's the state which tends to step in and ensure that they can be carried through. The long history of seemingly arbitrary and punitive anti-strike measures in the UK are testament to this.

Baccaro and Howell's data start in the mid-1970s and go up to 2005, showing that this market-centred 'conversion' of labour-market institutions had been in swing for decades by the time of the 2008 financial crisis. This crisis was not caused by an over-privileged working class or the absence of a labour force adapted to the needs of employers. Indeed, there is good evidence that the weakening of workers' bargaining power since the 1980s had contributed to economic crises by fuelling consumer reliance on debt in the absence of rising wages, thus destabilizing the finance system (Stockhammer and Onaran, 2012).

And yet, in the crisis' aftermath, austerity and marketization continued to be imposed even more forcefully across Europe. Look at Greece, where non-market institutions were brutally dismantled. Privatizations were violently enforced, collective bargaining institutions demolished and the minimum wage reduced. The absolutely predictable result was a collapse in living standards and the 'financial waterboarding' of the economy. The idea that this was the best route to an economically and politically stable Greece is, to put it mildly, questionable.

The second half of the book will deal with this puzzle of real-world marketization, showing its extremely diverse forms. It is not driven by external shocks, and it is not a result of sticky policy systems. It has been engineered by central governments seeking to impose changes on their own societies. These initiatives often clash with existing arrangements within these societies, and in such cases, the role of the state becomes even more important in forcing these shifts through. Moreover, they do not only disrupt, deregulate and liberalize, but they also are often institutionally thick, bureaucratically bloated and intended to improve coordination and control. The theories discussed earlier are inadequate to explaining the changes taking place. For alternatives, we draw inspiration from Marxist theory, which we use in adapted form.

Financialization and class discipline

Marxist writing about the state starts from a very different point from the political science literature discussed previously. The basic assumption underpinning it is that the state is essentially on the side of capital and thus opposed to the interests of workers. While political scientists may attempt to explain the conditions under which business interests are more likely to succeed, the class bias of capitalist states is axiomatic for Marxists. But what does it actually mean?

It might simply be taken to mean that the elites who run the state are more sympathetic to the concerns of capitalists rather than those of workers. This argument was made by influential twentieth-century Marxists such as Ralph Miliband. These authors were often building on the work of Antonio Gramsci, the Italian intellecctual who died following political persecution in Mussolini's Italy. For Gramsci, a key question was the way in which certain segments of the wider capitalist class are able to exercise influence over the state. Particular groups of capitalists could win wide consent for policies that would benefit them, by successfully framing their priorities as synonymous with the 'general interest'.

The Gramscian line of thinking has definite similarities with the political science literature discussed earlier, albeit with a Marxist twist. Gramscian writers, like theorists of policy systems, are primarily concerned with the way different interest groups exercise disproportionate influence over governments. What distinguishes them is that in Gramscian thinking it's not just abstract groups or 'actors' that compete for influence: it's specific social classes (e.g. Plehwe et al., 2007). When particular class groups become sufficiently influential, their needs start to become perceived as not just their own, but as what is best for everyone. Consequently, the actions of the state tend to be decided with the interests of this group in mind. To study the state from this perspective, is therefore to focus on the political, intellectual, cultural and ideological ways in which sections of the capitalist class come to occupy a position of leadership in society, and how this can be challenged.

Miliband's (1969) theory of the capitalist state works differently. For him, control over the state is highly personalized. There tends to be a personal affinity between business elites and state officials which is not extended to other groups, such as trade unionists. People in these networks may have the same social circles, similar upbringings and consequently similar worldviews. They are on the same wavelength, which effectively excludes everyone else from influence. If anyone wants to shape the direction of the state, they have to become part of this elite scene. And in doing so, they will inevitably start to feel pressure to conform to the status quo, since they will increasingly embody it. From this point of view, the election of a radical political party to government would not really change very much.

In a well-known debate with Miliband, Nicos Poulantzas argued that personal affinities and interconnections between state and capitalist elites failed to explain much at all about how the state works. This personalized type of analysis, focused on the sordid links and affinities between different branches of the elites, in his view, was rather gossipy and trivial. Instead, he advised viewing the state as a 'material condensation' of class relations.[1] Through the state, conflicts of interest between labour and capital are frozen and contained within a formalized institutional setting, as mediated, for instance, by political parties who come to act as conduits for different interest groups. From the perspective of capitalist elites, this is generally 'safer' than the alternative, which might be open conflict within workplaces, which would jeopardize the process of production and exchange.

An example of how this works can be found in the changes in the capitalist state that occurred after the Second World War, including the growth of welfare institutions and the proliferation of policies to encourage collective bargaining. From a Poulantzasian perspective, these changes should be seen as a 'condensation' of the rising class power of labour throughout the 1950s and 1960s. Due to increasing demand for labour in this period, workers were able to command more rights and drive relatively rapid wage growth. This could be quite worrying from capital's point of view. But in fact, in developed capitalist countries across the world, labour's class power was channelled into a series of formal institutions with their own procedural rules.

These institutions acted as a box to contain working-class power within manageable parameters, preventing it from getting out of control. The welfare state and extensive collective bargaining helped meet workers' aspirations for a better standard of living, while maintaining a relatively compliant workforce and continued profitability. Alexander Gallas (2017), a follower of Poultanzas, gives another example: the creation of legal frameworks guaranteeing the rights of trade unions. This is attractive to workers. But it is also limiting because by accepting these institutional rights, workers' organizations

---

[1] For more depth on this point, see Poulantzas (2000). The following discussion of Poulantzas's work is also influenced by Gallas (2017), Barrow (1993) and Skocpol (1980).

also accept the constraints and obligations that come with them. They buy into a formalized process that follows 'predictable rituals' set down by the capitalist state. So the state does not simply ensure 'capitalist domination'; given how chaotic societies are, this is not really possible. Instead, it is a set of institutions which embody and crystallize class conflict, but in such a way that the possibility of more radical social transformation is largely defused.

The key theoretical point here is that the need to maintain stable capitalist production and exchange guides the decisions states make. But this is never a clear or simple process because at any given moment there are many different interest groups and demands being made of them. Capitalist societies are dynamic and often unpredictable, and so the task facing state actors is frequently bewildering. They have to address problems which are constantly shapeshifting, whether caused by increasing assertiveness by workers' movements after 1945 or the public health menace of a viral pandemic as in the early 2020s. But they have to do this in a way which doesn't jeopardize the dominance of capital over labour, since without this there is no capitalism. So there is always a deep tension and instability underpinning the development of institutions and the making of policy by the state. This means that the role of the state is often very messy. Many of its initiatives are likely to be quite dysfunctional, creating confusion and conflict.

It's important to note an obvious limit to this argument. It doesn't tell us much at all about the actual *content* of the policies being introduced. It is one thing to say that capitalist state institutions contain and condense class conflict. But our question is different: Why has the specific agenda of marketization become so important to states, even when it jeopardizes stability? Miliband's analysis of personal networks of concentrated power is not much help here. A Poulantzasian focus on the dysfunctional institutions of state may be of more use, but it needs to be equipped with some modifications.

Marxist state theory sheds light on the wider political-economic context in which states are acting. To understand marketization, however, we also need to understand how states have increasingly seen class discipline as an end in itself, to be elevated above other goals such as maintaining a stable and coherent institutional system. And the reason for this shift is developments in the international political economic environment, including the ever-weaker threat posed to capital by organized labour and concurrent trends towards greater financialization. By financialization, we mean the increasing importance of financial rather than productive investments as a source of profits and economic activity, the international mobility of these investments via financial markets, and the growing imperative for firms to demonstrate 'shareholder value' (i.e. profitability in the short term) in order to attract investment from highly mobile capital.

In the vast research literature on financialization, it is often argued that the rising power of finance pushes businesses into a more short-termist focus on immediate profitability at the expense of longer-term organizational development (Lazonick and O'Sullivan, 2000) with often devastating consequences for workers and firms (Appelbaum and Batt, 2014). Financialization undermines the power of the working class, not only because it is more mobile than productive capital, but also because it is less subject to disruption or influence by organized workers (Lapavitsas, 2013). Financial investments can be moved around more quickly, and because finance capital tends to seek out opportunities for profit in the near future, its movement is unpredictable and subject to influences which may be more opaque and psychologically driven.[2] Vogl (2014) writes that this makes it very hard to predict how price signals are going to evolve or fluctuate, making them appear more or less random at times. Instead, there is a very diffuse sense that companies and governments need to win the 'confidence' of financial markets in order to attract investment (Aglietta, 2000). What this would actually entail in practice often appears quite subjective and hard to evidence.

How does this comment on financialization affect the role of the state in marketization processes? It matters, because it shows how difficult

---

[2] For critical commentary on this aspect of finance and capitalism in Marxist thought, see Harvey (2018) and De Brunhoff (2016).

it has become for capitalist states to secure stability and economic growth. Financialization disrupts states' abilities to plan the growth of their economies. It makes them more dependent on winning 'business confidence', but it becomes less and less clear what this means (Barta and Johnston, 2018). The scope for dysfunctional policymaking is thus greatly magnified. And it's in this context that class discipline comes to the fore.

States and class discipline

Using Poulantzas's theory, the institutions developed during the mid-twentieth century for protecting workers from the effects of market competition – collective bargaining, pro-worker regulations, expansion of the public sector and the welfare state – are a crystallization of the balance of power between labour and capital that emerged after the Second World War. Organized labour was relatively strong in this period. By facilitating the creation of these institutions, the state both reflected that balance and contained it within a stable set of mechanisms so as to reduce the possibility of a more radical challenge to the structure of capitalist societies.

This arrangement – often referred to as a kind of 'class compromise' or 'social compact' (e.g. Daguerre, 2014) – needed a degree of stability to work. The post-war system in developed capitalist countries, for a period of thirty years or so, had a kind of internal order to it: rising wages and strengthened job security fit with industrial mass production because they provided an expanding national market to ensure growth. This dynamic could also be maintained because the short-term logic of shareholder value was less prevalent. Matt Vidal (2013) calls this a 'functional accumulation regime'. In this relatively stable international context, the role of the state in regulating class conflict is easier to envision. But after the 1970s, Vidal argues this gave way to a 'dysfunctional accumulation regime', characterized by outsourcing, intensified international competition and financialization. The opacity and short-termism of financialized capital, as we argued in the last section, greatly hinders the maintenance of a stable and cohesive set of state institutions.

Class discipline, we argue, is a common strategy through which governments have responded to this shifting context. Coherent institutional systems, which can regulate capitalist production and contain class conflict within a stable national economy, give way to an urgent need to compete for fast-moving international investment. This, in turn, gives rise to a pre-eminent focus on ensuring 'business confidence' as a policy priority. This confidence is intangible, and it is notoriously difficult for states to reliably predict what kinds of policy will bolster it. Often, it is mediated through institutions like credit ratings agencies, who themselves use relatively opaque criteria but tend to dislike governments they imagine might allow democratic political choices to interfere with market freedoms (Sinclair, 1994; Barta and Johnston, 2018).

Consequently, we argue that governments have increasingly treated class discipline as an end in itself. More and more, the creation of a compliant working population, with lower expectations about work quality and weaker trade unions, becomes a policy objective. Influential politicians who have featured in our story are often quite open about this; it's just that they use different language. When the long-time Conservative politician Iain Duncan Smith, for instance, sold his coercive approach to welfare recipients as an attempt to instil a 'work ethic' and valorize the 'dignity of work' in the UK, it is no real reach to see this as a call for class discipline expressed in alternative language. For him, it was about a 'cultural change' in which people could discover a willingness to work in any available job.[3] This argument rules out any critical discussion of the *quality* of work: not just pay and job security, but whether workers have opportunities to negotiate over how their industry is run, whether they have institutions like unions to represent

---

[3] For a hymn to Duncan Smith's services to class discipline, see *London Evening Standard* (2012).

their interests or whether they can access training and develop skills. All of this is of no real interest; what matters is simply that people are *willing to work under whatever conditions the market offers.*

Iain Duncan Smith is a conveniently odious spokesperson for the work ethic, but he is not alone, and the 'Anglo-Saxon' world is not unusual for featuring this kind of rhetoric. Our German interviewees from 2003 to 2004 were angry about rhetoric from the government about claimants as 'social parasites' who preferred hammocks to the job search. Emmanuel Macron is lauded by an English Conservative commentator for his embrace of the 'Protestant work ethic', which boils down to the strikingly simple maxim: shut up and work harder (Heffer, 2020). One of his predecessors expressed the aim of organizing 'a festival of real work' to honour those who 'suffer' in their jobs without complaining, as a kind of counterweight to the indiscipline of trade union activists demanding more (Reuters, 2012). In the next chapter we will show how, at the EU level, 'activating the inactive', in other words, the recalibration of welfare systems to prioritize forcing people into work irrespective of its quality, has become an increasingly urgent priority.

It is striking how durable these ideas are (see McCallum, 2020). Even during a global pandemic which has been greatly exacerbated by people crowding together in workplaces and on commuter journeys, few mainstream politicians have argued for a cultural shift away from work and towards more leisure time, and there has in many cases been a pronounced desire to return to the status quo ante with regard to work and labour-market arrangements. You can't see your families, and you can't have visitors in your house or garden, but you still have to work, whatever the consequences for public health. We will return to this theme later.

Our point here is not about the cultural blather of the 'work ethic'. The point is to underline that, when we say governments are preoccupied by class discipline, this should not be read as Marxist paranoia. It's really just a way of describing the same ideas that political elites shove in front of us on a daily basis. We are just drawing out its implications.

And it is in this context that we can finally return to marketization itself. To explain the curious persistence of marketization, we need to understand this class disciplinary context. Marketization might be chaotic and hard work. It might reduce service quality and fair to improve the outcomes of public policies. It might be expensive and bureaucratic. But it has other benefits, as we will show in detail in Chapters 4–6 of this book. First, it is a potent means of disciplining workers. Second, its institutional mechanics have enabled capital to protect itself from this same discipline. Third, it has insulated these mechanics from democratic oversight. The latter, evidently, is also a kind of class discipline but a kind which acts on entire societies, rather than specific groups of workers.

Capitalist states and marketization in a pandemic

At the time of writing (early 2022), it is still too early to say with certainty what the Covid-19 pandemic means for the subject of this book. But it would also be odd to ignore it. What does marketization mean for Covid-19? What does Covid-19 mean for marketization? Our answers will necessarily be quite speculative.

One of the common responses on the left to the first question is to argue that marketization has enfeebled societies and left them unable to cope with the gravity of the situation, a comment frequently made of marketized health systems in particular. Marketizing policies, some have argued, reduced hospital capacity and introduced new incentive systems that were inappropriate to coping with Covid-19. We dig into this further in Chapter 5.

This kind of argument is sometimes transposed onto a much wider scale. Pankaj Mishra (2020), for instance, writes that the pandemic has underlined the failings of the 'Anglo-American' world. He claims that their ideological dependence on markets partly explains why they appear to have dealt with Covid-19 conspicuously worse than more 'statist' societies such as China and South Korea. But there are big dangers in making an argument that is so broad brush. We have argued earlier against juxtaposing 'market' and 'state', since engineering market competition often involves expanding the state.

Moreover, it's not yet possible to reliably divide up the world into countries which have handled Covid-19 well and those which have handled it badly. Although some success stories and some demonstrable failures can be identified, these don't produce neat conclusions (Watkins, 2020). Some clownish populist governments have botched the handling of Covid-19, but so have some technocratic liberal ones, including the institutions of the European Union. The dynamics in any given place are the product of the many factors that shape local situations.

Identifying the effects of marketization on countries' responses to the pandemic requires a fine-grained analysis, not country-by-country, but sector-by-sector and policy-by-policy. Class disciplinary policies normally look short-sighted in the context of the pandemic, and this is not only because market mechanisms are unhelpful in preparing health systems for a pandemic. When welfare systems are oriented towards pushing people into work under any circumstances, and when workers' ability to address the quality of that work is undermined, there are public health consequences. People show up to work where health and safety provisions are inadequate, because they haven't been able to negotiate improvements, and because the welfare system does not recognize their right to decline work. Susan Watkins (2020), looking at Latin America, argues that the weak welfare system in Peru is one reason its Covid-19 problems have exceeded even those in Brazil (whose government's disastrous response has achieved much greater international attention). In the latter, welfare support has been made significantly more robust since Lula's Presidency, thus mitigating the problems caused by Bolsonaro's Covid-denial. Adams-Prassl and colleagues (2020), examining the UK, find that 43 per cent of workers without access to sick pay would 'definitely go to work with a cold or light fever'. When workers are unable to negotiate improvements in the quality and safety of their workplace, employers can more easily cram them into cramped working conditions without adequate protections, even at the height of lockdowns (Malet, 2020). In many situations a tension thus exists between class discipline and effective infection prevention.

Now we can turn to the second question. What will marketization look like after Covid-19? States have initiated programmes to limit unemployment and provide support for struggling industries during the pandemic. Already, there is discussion of 'how this will be paid for', a question no less likely to be raised by right-wing governments than by centre–left politicians desperate to appear suitably pro-business. Recent history suggests that the main strategy will be to pay back creditors and cut public spending.

But this doesn't simply mean an endless future of austerity and marketization. These two things, in fact, have a complicated relationship. As we will show in our discussion of health and welfare, when services are starved for funds, low prices make it difficult to organize competition. It's not very lucrative for private companies enter 'austerity markets' (Gingrich, 2011). The institutional mechanics of marketization will probably be set back by Covid-19, if it produces resource scarcity in health and welfare markets.

But this doesn't mean that the will to marketize will have been reduced. Just because marketization initiatives may prove inefficient and underwhelming doesn't mean governments will lose interest. Post-pandemic, it would not be surprising if class discipline emerges as an even greater priority in many countries. Newspapers and government briefings will be full of discussion about the workers who 'benefited' from furlough schemes and labour shortages, and who now need to make amends by working extra hard to help their cash-strapped employers. This is particularly important where workers' wage demands, in various sectors, appear to be rising; where many workers have quit jobs in sectors such as retail owing to poor conditions combined with heightened health risks; and where workers appear more inclined to protest (Trappmann et al., 2022). There is a glimpse of a shift in the balance of power between labour and capital, and marketization is one likely policy response.

Indeed, the pursuit of class discipline that goes hand-in-hand with marketization has not gone away, even at the height of worldwide lockdowns. Iain Duncan Smith, for instance, rejected calls for a more universalist welfare system on the grounds that it would produce a 'disincentive to work' (Stone, 2020). The making of this argument at the same moment workplaces were acting as vectors for a catastrophic virus is something for us to merely note, and for future historians to marvel at. One of his media enablers, meanwhile, had a better idea: Why not introduce a Universal Basic Income, but in the form of a loan where, once Covid-19 has gone away, people have to pay it all back? (Peston, 2020). Meanwhile in the United States, the pandemic-era boost to unemployment insurance was allowed by a centre–left government to expire in September 2021 at a time when 2000 Americans per day were perishing from Covid-19, as an explicit response to employer difficulties recruiting low-wage workers (Stettner, 2021).

As we write, provisions afforded to the world's workers during the pandemic are ending, and the pre-pandemic norms of work-first social policy beckon. A pessimist might envision future waves of marketization in public services leading to further institutional confusion and unforeseen consequences, as the fashionable pandemic-era rhetoric about 'heroic' essential or key workers looks more and more hollow. Below we will ponder whether this is too gloomy. But suffice to say, even a global pandemic may not in the long run be enough to alter the class dynamics that have driven marketization.

Part II

Marketization in practice

4

The discipline of work

Marketization in welfare-to-work systems

Having set out some arguments in support of a critical theory of marketization in the first half of the book, we now examine concrete examples of marketization in practice, drawn from recent European political economy. We begin with a study of welfare-to-work systems, which provide a compelling illustration of the theoretical arguments we have made previously about marketization and class discipline.

Governments have long seen the labour market as a tool to reduce poverty and inequality. The classic methods include paying unemployed workers cash benefits while offering them job-search assistance through a public employment service. But some unemployed workers need more targeted services to find a job. Someone with a disability or illness may need medical services or adjustments to work arrangements; a worker lacking an important certification may need a training course; and workers with families may need help with childcare or elder care. Governments have increasingly combined these forms of support with compulsion, such as cash penalties, also known as sanctions, for not complying with the requirements attached to jobless benefits.

As in many areas of market change, the language is contested and confusing. Critical social science often uses the term 'workfarism' to describe a welfare state that uses punishments to enforce requirements for jobless people to actively seek work, while also using market pressures to reorganize services. Policymakers have increasingly turned to punitive Active Labor Market Policies (ALMPs), in which supports are combined with punishments to push jobless people back into paid work.

For some idea of what we mean by punishment, consider the abolition of Incapacity Benefits (IB) in Britain that started in 2007. A Labour government commissioned a study by economist Paul Gregg, which noted the damaging effects of joblessness on health and the desire of many disabled people to go back to work. His recommendations included abolishing IB, reassessing existing claimants, changing the assessment process for new claimants, and creating a new benefit known as the Employment Support Allowance (ESA). To receive ESA, some claimants would be subject to job-search requirements, backed up by sanctions. The new system would identify and support job-ready people, the theory went, and their well-being would improve once they were included in the world of work (Gregg, 2008).

The implementation of this policy was dramatized in the Ken Loach film, *I, Daniel Blake*. After a heart attack, the main character, a widowed elderly carpenter who lives in the northeast of England, is told by a doctor that he needs to quit working while he recovers. The contractor that carries out assessments of ESA claimants, the multinational IT firm Atos Origen, rejects his claim based on a telephone interview. The film tells of his struggle to survive, including his appeal of the ruling by Atos, his signing on to job-seeker benefits, his attempts to comply with job-search requirements, his benefits sanctions by the job centre and his arrest by the police after a series of dehumanizing encounters with the benefits system. At the end of the film, just as his appeal is heard, he dies of a heart attack.

The film was made in 2015, while we were doing our research in Britain and at a time when claimants groups, trade unionists and others were pushing back against the government's punitive policies towards the jobless. The reform of disability benefits was a particularly egregious example of punishing the poor, since it had a quantifiable death toll. The government objected to the film, but it also produced a statistical report showing that 2,380 people had died shortly after being declared fit for work between December 2011 and February 2014 alone (Department for Work and Pensions, 2015). One claimants' group, the Black Triangle Campaign, was formed in 2010 after the Scottish poet

Paul Reeky committed suicide with two letters laid in front of him: notices that he had been denied for housing benefit and for incapacity benefit. Activists from dozens of local groups around the country demonstrated at Atos offices, making it a 'toxic brand' (as one Atos worker told us), and leading the company to pull out of the contract to deliver the assessments.

Activism against Britain's punitive reforms was not limited to the reform of incapacity benefits. A similar policy was pursued towards lone parents of small children receiving Income Support. The Public and Commercial Services Union (PCS), which has a membership density of 80 per cent in the job centres, exposed other problems as well: the escalating number of sanctions of claimants of mainstream job-seeker benefits, the use of sanctions to enforce participation in work-for-benefits schemes ('workfare' in the strict sense) and the expectation by some supervisors that front-line advisors levy sanctions (PCS, 2014). Moreover, contracting with Britain's public employment service was a lucrative business, especially for the owners of for-profit service providers who won large contracts and then sold their businesses. The owners of Ingeus UK, Britain's largest Work Programme contractor, sold out to a US firm in 2014, pocketing US\$ 225 million in an up-front payment plus additional millions subject to subsequent performance.[1]

Although the case of Britain is intriguing, with its death toll and rampant profiteering, it is not unique. The United States played a pioneering role in modern punishments for the poor, starting in the 1970s with 'workfare'. This reform was aimed at a specific group of claimants – mostly single mothers claiming Aid to Families with Dependent Children and then Temporary Assistance for Needy Families – and had little impact on mainstream unemployment or disability benefits. Germany's Hartz reforms were much further-reaching,

---

[1] This and other details on marketized employment services in the UK, Germany and Denmark can be found in Greer et al. (2017). For more on alternative forms of governance, see Jantz et al. (2018).

combining social assistance and unemployment assistance with a single means-tested benefit with strict work requirements and sanctions. In Slovenia, which has not yet turned to widespread sanctioning, the government encourages precarious work through social activation programs for vulnerable groups and benefits top-ups for claimants who do volunteer work. We will show further that the conditions attached to jobless benefits have increased over time internationally, while the generosity of supports – both cash benefits and support services – has tended to decline.

'Activation' does not have to be punitive and coercive. Workers would benefit from a well-functioning public employment service offering specialized assistance depending on their particular needs. In France, we observed a kind of active labour-market scheme that emphasized empowerment of clients and resisted sanctions or profiteering (Schulte et al., 2018). But across Europe, in example after example, policies that are supposed to address the social exclusion of jobless people end up inflicting class discipline on workers.

A dual marketization process

Punitive active labour-market policies involve marketization on two interlocking levels. First, they push jobless people into the labour market, including people with severe difficulties searching for and keeping jobs. In doing so, they intensify competition in the labour market by coercing people to enter it and using sanctions to frighten workers who otherwise might suspend their job search. To put it in the language we used previously, this is therefore a way of forcibly expanding market entry. Second, they intensify competition among the organizations and workers who deliver activation services, using public-management tools such as vouchers and competitive tendering to simulate a market for clients or for contracts (Greer, 2016). As we will see, these two marketization processes reinforce each other.

The task of 'activating' the jobless is not simply a matter of maintaining a public employment service, sending unemployed people on courses and paying for their bus tickets to their next jobs. The national-level policymakers who design ALMPs have limited knowledge of employer skill demands in each local labour market, the skills and other attributes of job seekers or even the training and advice services that supposedly implement their policy. The labour markets they are facing change with the business cycle, the rise and decline of certain occupations and industries, local demographic shifts and workplace changes that determine employer skill requirements. Front-line workers and their line managers administering ALMPs have a strong intuitive sense of the labour market from their daily conversations with employers and job seekers, and traditionally they had considerable discretion in using this knowledge in their work (Rothstein, 1998; Finn, 2000).

Beyond the contingencies of labour-market conditions, the job of activation is further complicated by the circumstances of service users. Front-line workers are up against the so-called barriers to work of their clients, such as addiction, caring responsibilities, criminal records, debt, disability, domestic violence, homelessness, inadequate or not recognized formal qualifications, discrimination from employers on the basis of age, disability, ethnicity, gender, race, mental illness, transportation problems, and much more. Their clients often face many of these barriers at the same time, and the problem is exacerbated by austerity policies that cut public services that could help them access paid work. Consequently, the front-line work of assisting job seekers requires time, flexibility and professional skills.

Many jobless people who claim benefits are not 'unemployed' according to the definitions used by government statistics offices. While unemployment implies an active job search and availability for work, many jobless people are temporarily unavailable or incapable for searching for work due to training or medical treatment, caring responsibilities, or because they could catch a deadly virus during a pandemic and pass it on to vulnerable family members. (In the film, Daniel Blake had to actively search for work in order to collect Jobseekers

Allowance, even though he was unavailable to work due to his heart condition.) Other claimants of benefits have jobs, but they are part-time and low-wage; the benefits system considers them underemployed and tops up their wages. Also potentially affected by punitive workfare incentives are unemployed workers who are not available for the low-wage jobs on offer; these workers often have high levels of education and specialized skills and face long spells of unemployment while they compete for scarce jobs with pay and status commensurate with their experience. Often the system requires them to apply for the much more numerous entry-level jobs or jobs outside of their field, where their skills are irrelevant.

Even setting aside the misery caused by sanctioning, the results of ALMPs have often been poor. Front-line workers in job centres do not have the power or resources to address the many inequities in the labour market that make it difficult to place their clients in sustained jobs. Their task has been described as 'Sisyphean' by one authority, who notes the self-defeating effects of classifying clients using a 'handicapology', a language that both expresses and reinforces their distance from the labour market (Castel, 2017). One early advocate for ALMPs, Günther Schmid (2008), called the evaluation evidence on their work 'disappointing', and after decades of experimentation, the outcomes of ALMPs remain mixed and an overall assessment of their economic impact has been elusive at best (Card et al., 2018). The work of job placement and administering benefits is made difficult by poor job quality, that is when jobs are temporary and pay poverty wages, and clients cycle between unemployment, activation schemes and temporary jobs.[2]

One way governments have responded to the mediocre performance of ALMPs has been to use marketization initiatives to change how services are governed and delivered. Instead of simply paying public-

---

[2] For a pandemic-era meditation on this problem, see Greer et al. (2021). For a German view directly after the Hartz reforms, see Dörre et al. (2013).

sector workers or covering the costs of non-profits in advising and training jobless people, governments have increasingly used competitive tendering and vouchers. This has led to the rise of for-profit service providers skilled in winning these contracts, and the professionalization and commercialization of the non-profit sector. It also involves fixing the length of contracts to ensure market transactions are conducted regularly and frequently and opening services up to new, especially for-profit, providers. This is why we refer at the start of this section to a dual marketization: marketization acts not only on service users themselves but also on the organizations delivering these schemes.

When governments adopt competitive tendering, they reconfigure the transactions through which organizations are engaged to provide employment services. Instead of paying a non-profit or public organization to cover their costs, governments start to use time-limited contracts that specify a price for a particular defined service or outcome, thus increasing the frequency of transactions, and introducing a framework for comparing market participants. Since the Hartz reforms, Germany's public employment service has created a well-resourced purchasing function to buy training courses or job-placement schemes, using an algorithm to compare the price and quality of offers. For any given scheme, every twelve to thirty-six months, the contract ends and an opportunity opens up to change service providers. Most managers of providers we visited reported that they had been undercut by a competitor offering a similar but lower-quality service for a lower price. The managers who run the purchasing function argued in interviews that a standardized scoring system was a fairer and more objective way to evaluate bid documents that reduced the political considerations often associated with funding non-profits. The purchasing centres of Germany's employment services negotiate thousands of contracts every year.

Britain has used competitive tendering to re-engineer services in a different way: creating a centralized market for employment services with larger and longer-term contracts, dominated by for-profit firms. This market was put in place after the 2010 election by the recently elected Conservative government, but built on a decade of incremental changes made by Labour governments. The vast majority of non-profit and municipal agencies that had previously been funded directly by central government to provide services became subcontractors for large companies managing large contracts covering territories the size of Scotland, Wales or East London. Unlike German competitive tendering, the aim was not mainly to tightly control the contractor through frequent retendering and detailed specification of work. Instead, the British system used payment by results, combined with light-touch regulation, to stimulate innovation.

At the outset of the Work Programme, providers competed based on price to participate in the program, but this competition was not as relentless as in Germany due to the long contract, and the main for-profit providers had flexibility to reduce their own spending or to shift costs and risks onto subcontractors via performance management. These large contractors were shielded from competitive pressures because they enjoyed infrequent transactions and a contracting procedure that refrained from spelling out the service in detail. However, they did have the opportunity to ratchet up competitive pressure on their own subcontractors. In the first eighteen months of the Work Programme, about 35 per cent of subcontractors had their contracts cancelled by a prime contractor (Greer et al., 2017: 94). The latter thus became agents of marketization themselves and could orchestrate competition lower down the food chain, while being cushioned from the risks. This is another reminder that marketization and market concentration are not opposite ends of a spectrum.

Another approach to marketizing employment services has been the use of vouchers. This means giving service users a document that they can use to access services that the service provider can redeem for a payment. Unlike with competitive tendering, where the government purchasing office decides on the provider, with vouchers, it is ostensibly the client who decides which service to use. Germany has voucher schemes both for training and job-placement services, where mostly for-profit firms compete for customers seeking assistance. Job centre staff supply job seekers with vouchers, which the training or placement companies can redeem after the service is complete. Evaluations show that voucher schemes put strains on relationships between the public-sector funder and private-sector provider, and that because of a lack of information in the market they do not normally offer job seekers a meaningful 'customer choice' (Hipp and Warner, 2008). But by intensifying competition for clients, voucher systems do create considerable uncertainty for service providers, who, we found in Germany, shifted that uncertainty onto workers by hiring them on temporary contracts or on a freelance basis.

Market discipline operates here at multiple levels. On job seekers, it is enforced by front-line workers in employment services who are themselves increasingly subject to market discipline. The result is a system that forces jobless people to compete for low-wage jobs in an inequitable labour market, providing support services of ever-diminishing quality and quantity. This is a grim situation, especially for those who spend months unsuccessfully looking for work and who may, like Daniel Blake, be incapable of genuinely competing on the labour market. They exacerbate, among other things, stress-related medical conditions (Williams, 2021), often with fatal consequences. These pressures may also force the job-ready to reduce their expectations in terms of job quality just to escape from the system. But there is also another level of marketization: that operating on providers themselves. This dimension of marketization disciplines the front-line workers charged with delivering these services. As we will show in the next section, for the social workers, trainers and advisors charged with supporting service users, there is less job security and less job autonomy, along with fewer resources to support clients and ever more reasons to issue sanctions. The result is what these markets should in theory prevent – large numbers of job seekers who could use assistance are simply neglected.

Creaming and parking

The main intellectual justification for marketization in public services has been Julian Le Grand's (2003) theory of 'quasi-markets'. This school of thought sees public-sector bureaucracy as populated by self-interested individuals who are normally unresponsive to the needs and desires of service users (patients, clients or customers). Front-line workers need market discipline for the system to respond to users' needs. Unlike most true believers in the market and adherents to the Goldilocks view, quasi-market theory recognizes that the government ultimately decides how the market will function. Governments determine the pricing of services, the mix of private and non-profit entities that compete for funds to deliver services, and the incentives that result.

One notable effort to implement these ideas has been the aforementioned shift towards competitive tendering in British employment services. The architect of these changes, an investment banker named David Freud (incidentally, Sigmund's great-grandson), published a report in 2007, commissioned by a Labour government, to create an employment services market. The Freud Report (2007) criticized past privatization efforts as too prescriptive, describing in detail the service to be performed, and paid not according to outcomes but according to activities undertaken. Instead of paying for unemployed people to spend a fixed number of hours in classes or being coached (known in the industry as 'bums on seats'), the Freud Report argued that government should pay for job outcomes and give private service providers the flexibility they would need to innovate. Contracts should be large and long-lasting so that managers could plan and investors could achieve a return, potentially attracting capital from the finance sector. An incentive structure should be created that encourages service providers to focus attention on the neediest service users by creating a higher price tag for their job outcomes than for someone who is obviously job-ready. The incentive structure should discourage, he said, 'creaming and parking' (where providers concentrate on the job-ready and neglect clients with more complex barriers to work) but should encourage private investors to finance the organizations that would deliver the services.

Freud's vision was fully embraced by the conservative-led government after the 2010 general election, which moved quickly to cancel most contracted-out schemes (notably the 'New Deals'), spending millions of pounds to buy them out. It then created the Work Programme, which combined the clienteles of most of the previous schemes, ranging from average job seekers that had been unemployed for fifty-two weeks or more to former claimants of IB whose spell of joblessness had lasted several years. Depending on the kind of benefit and the age of the claimant, providers could be paid a maximum ranging from £3700 to £13,720 for a sustained job outcome (paid in thirteen to twenty-six four-week increments). Crucially, the contract was a 'black box'. This meant, to allow innovation, the contractor itself – that is those large commercially minded organizations that contracted directly with central government and contracted out some of the work to smaller organizations – was responsible for defining the work. Service quality was defined in terms of outcome quantity, that is sustained jobs. Thus, great efforts were taken to entice new actors into the marketplace, at the expense of other market requirements such as transaction frequency.

We visited several of these contractors' offices as they were rolling out the Work Programme, and – given the rationale of 'black box' contracting as promoting innovation – they were surprisingly standardized. Near the entrance was a desk with a porter who greeted clients, as well as a computer lab where they could search for jobs. Past the porter was an open-plan office with computer terminals where most meetings between advisors and clients would take place. Just off these spaces were separate rooms for group interviews, training sessions and confidential meetings. The combination of resource scarcity, payment by results and discretion for management created a clear incentive structure to which commercial providers could respond. As one executive described it,

> so you get less people into work, and because you're getting less people into work you target, and because it's outcome based, you're going to target your resources at those people who are easiest to help. So you're going to aggressively park and cream. You cream by targeting the easy ones, you park by identifying the people you can't help and ignore them. (Greer et al., 2017: 150)

Any new client would undergo a quick assessment for job readiness. If he or she was deemed job-ready, then they would be put in one group (often 'green'); if there were barriers to employment they would be put in one of two other groups (often 'red' or 'amber', depending on the severity of these barriers). The green group would be sent to staff who would prepare them for interviews with employers, while red and amber clients would be sent to support services, if they were available. Because there was little funding for these services – social services were being cut back across the public sector during this period – more often they would receive an email or phone call periodically from an advisor, the so-called 'minimum service'. The promises to clients put into the bids and published online included vague promises, such as 'we will keep in regular contact with you'; descriptions of processes, such as a timeline for induction and assessments; and in a few cases concrete pledges, such the promise of a 'named advisor', monthly meetings with advisors, 'contact' fortnightly or monthly, or 'a service that is accessible to all on public transport within 30–45 minutes' (Greer et al., 2017: 72–73).

These minimum standards left much space for the neglect of clients, with workers telling us that they simply did not have the time or resources to assist many of them, except to direct them to the computer labs where they could independently take online courses and look at online job advertisements. One front-line worker we met had a caseload of more than 200 'red' clients. Another pointed to the computer lab and said, 'if this isn't parking, I don't know what is!' This whole process, from assessment, to job placement, to sustaining that job placement over two years, was overseen by an elaborate electronic system used for reporting outcomes to government and managing the performance of staff (Greer et al., 2018).

Alongside the obvious consequences for service users, the status and roles of front-line workers who delivered services were changing. Rather than acting as professional providers of social services, with discretion over how to support vulnerable service users, they were now bound into systems of tight new rules and incentives in which there was no room for these professional skills. Automated systems told them who should be sanctioned and why, and new incentive structures squeezed out any notion of tailored support for individuals.

The Work Programme was governed with an eye to shifting risk, responsibility and power from the public sector into the for-profit sector. This included not only the management of front-line staff and design of services; it also included the management of relations with the non-profit sector. In an important sense, the Freud concept, as implemented in the Work Programme, recast the relationship between central government and civil society as a matter of supply-chain management. It was these firms that were deciding how employment support systems should be designed and how benefits claimants should be treated, rather than subjecting these questions to democratic scrutiny. Incidentally, these for-profit firms were exempt from public purchasing law, freeing them from the principles of transparency and equal treatment built into European competition law that government purchasers were bound by. (One European Commission staffer told us that the Procurement Directive exempted contractors, because its drafters assumed that for-profit firms were more efficient than the public sector and therefore needed less oversight.)

Non-profit providers and municipalities in which workers and managers opposed creaming and parking faced financial strain, because they had to cross-subsidize any support for clients who would otherwise be parked. Any democratic accountability, especially at the local level, gave way to the commercial considerations of the corporations running the Work Programme. Hence, the class and power dynamics of marketization in British workfare become clearer: there is a group of large for-profit firms who are able to insulate themselves from market discipline while orchestrating it among smaller organizations, imposing market discipline on service users and front-line workers.

The results of this system were as unimpressive as the schemes that came before. Outcomes for the job-ready were similar to previous schemes, but those for disabled people were much worse. This was not surprising: front-line staff, their line managers and executives were open with us about creaming and parking. Spending money on people who were seen as difficult to place in jobs was risky, and investors demanded a return. There were extremely strong commercial pressures on firms to cream and park. As audits of those organizations showed, providers spent less on young people and the disabled than they had planned. Instead, they focused their efforts on the job-ready, where they could claim outcome payments by placing job seekers who could find work with or without the service (National Audit Office, 2014). Another consequence of Britain's work-first employment services was that it became extremely difficult to reorient staff and providers in subsequent local projects to create less punitive services (Johnson et al., 2021).

Arguably, by encouraging 'parking', the Work Programme loosened the discipline on the working class, and compared to an intensive programme of behaviour modification, could be considered a form of benign neglect. It is true that many of the government's interventions whose ostensible purpose was to assist the unemployed in their job search shifted responsibility for unemployment onto the unemployed themselves, rebranding joblessness as a psychological disorder (Friedli and Stearn, 2015). And yet, even the clients 'parked' could be automatically sanctioned for infractions such as not appearing on-time to a meeting, and companies' electronic systems gave front-line advisors little discretion in the matter. As social policy scholar Jay Wiggan argues, the Work Programme was reasonably successful, not in terms of its 'ostensible' aims, but as an intervention by a capitalist state 'to manage labour power and buttress capital's authority' (Wiggan, 2015).

The neglect of clients was embedded in systems of punishment. The more difficulty a client had finding work, the more difficulty they would have complying with the conditions attached to their benefits. Sanctions do change the incentives facing job seekers. They are an effective way to increase hardship for those who do not succeed in the job search, especially for homeless people, disabled people, people with caring responsibility, people who face discrimination from employers because of their race or migration status, and other vulnerable groups. They can exacerbate health problems in life-threatening ways. One summary of the research evidence from the Joseph Rowntree Foundation lists the unintended consequences: 'distancing people from support; causing hardship and even destitution; displacing rather than resolving issues such as street homelessness and anti-social behaviour; and negative impacts on "third parties", particularly children' (Watts et al., 2014). These research studies, films such as *I Daniel Blake*, or mobilizations of workers and claimants against benefits, did not lead to a change in UK government sanctioning policy.[3] Indeed, our analysis of British public opinion using data from the International Social Survey Program since the 1980s shows that it has become increasingly hostile towards the unemployed and unemployment benefits (Coderre-LaPalme et al., 2021).

Activating the activators

The mixture of strict conditionality and corporate domination is not the only way to manage unemployment, but it is common internationally and certainly not confined to so-called Liberal Market Economies. In our studies across Europe, we observed a strong element of compulsion in Germany, Denmark and Britain as well as the marketization of employment services; and elements of workfarism have been found elsewhere in Europe (Lødemel and Moreira, 2014).

In Germany, for example, it was the public employment service that dominated services. It did so not only by virtue of the fact that it was the only funder but also through the way that it managed the transaction. Instead of privatizing governance by giving large firms control, the German public employment service created a well-resourced professional procurement function, as described above,

---

[3] Benefits sanctions rose and declined between 2010 and 2016; the decline was due to the end of the Work Programme and management practices within the ministry rather than official government policy. See Webster (2016).

for services purchased by local job centres. They defined the work in detail (which was excruciating from the perspective of some service providers) and used much smaller and shorter-term contracts. In doing so, they increased the frequency of transactions and provided a more precise brief to increase comparability between market participants. For-profit providers could not thrive in these circumstances due to the squeeze on prices and the difficulty of achieving large volumes of work. Hence, compared to Britain, German policy pushed the comparability and frequency dimensions of marketization, but were less generous when it came to incentivizing market entry. Purchasing officials in the German public employment service expressed shock when we described the policy in Britain of encouraging innovation through profit-making. One exclaimed, 'but that is public money'! However, although it was harder to realize profits in the German system, this did not lessen its disciplinary effects on service users or on front-line workers.

This competitive tendering system, many of our interviewees argued, tended to make the services more standardized, while also making it difficult to develop innovative and expensive services. One reason was that purchasing officials had created standard product descriptions that they could offer to job centres seeking to purchase services, saving the latter time that they might spend devising services and criteria for assessing bids. Another reason was the algorithm used to compare the price and quality assigned to bids. Bids could be excluded for falling below a certain threshold of quality points, and the bid with the highest ratio of quality to price did not automatically win. However, high-price bids were also excluded if their quality-to-price ratio was considerably lower than the leading one (normally by a fixed threshold amount such as 15 per cent). The scoring of bids also prevented providers from competing based on innovation, and the tendency of scorers to assess quality scores within a narrow range made price a more important distinguishing feature of bids. This very sophisticated algorithm not only created a fair and transparent (and above all procurement law-compliant) market, but it also wrongly treated quality and price as commensurable (see also Ferber, 2015). The result was to drain service providers of the resources and discretion they needed to innovate.

A clear contrast to the German and British approaches to marketization was the system of services for disadvantaged job seekers we observed in the Parisian suburbs, known as *insertion sociale*. The network of providers there has evolved since the 1980s in tandem with the evolution of the safety net benefits *Revenu minimum d'insertion* and *Revenu de solidarité active*, which have never fully taken on board the logic of compulsion or punishment. The reason for this is that local policymakers and front-line workers still had considerable control over the nature of services and the way they were delivered.

We first began approaching these organizations in 2012, after reading and hearing that the French welfare state had avoided the punitive turn taken in Germany (Barbier and Knuth, 2011), and being tipped off that one of the big multinational firms was establishing a presence in France. The contrast with Britain and Germany was immediately evident. Our attempts to set up interviews were initially frustrated by the local organizations' tendency not to return emails or answer their phones. But when we visited the Parisian suburbs (in the *département* Seine-Saint-Denis) and knocked on the doors, we met executive directors of mostly small organizations who spoke with us for 60–90 minutes without an appointment. Beyond the less frenetic pace of work, there were several differences (Schulte et al., 2018).

First, local policymakers and front-line workers had much greater control over the way services were provided. Instead of shifting decision-making power into a centralized purchasing office or a supply-chain management function, these services were devised by local and regional funders, through discussion with representatives of unemployment insurance funds, the public employment service, and non-profit service providers. This was the result of a decades-long process of decentralization and deconcentration of authority from what had previously been aloof and all-powerful government ministries (Bezes and Le Lidec, 2011). These 'decentralized' networks of local actors were charged with designing programmes of work and selecting schemes for young people, and 'deconcentrated' government ministries moved some of their decision-makers into the regions to become part of these networks. The services were supported by large amounts of funding to address inequities, which made international headlines during a 2005 wave of social unrest. Contracts to provide services were still time-limited, but in practice, managers at small provider organizations tended to feel secure in the knowledge that their contracts would be renewed. When a policy change came along (such as a request by local government to prioritize a particular kind of person for support), this would be discussed with existing providers in order to modify the services they were already providing, rather than leading to a new process of competitive tendering. Payment by results had, at the time of our interviews, been resisted. Organizations were typically paid according to the number of clients they served, rather than outcomes such as job placements.

The French system is fragmented, as the people who provide these employment services normally work in a separate agency from those who administer benefits. Unlike Britain or Germany, there is no central government body that coordinates services by controlling all the funding streams. This lack of 'integration' between the unemployment system and other social services (see Berthet and Bourgeois, 2016) may be a problem from the perspective of government ministers hoping to ramp up coercive activation and intensify market competition, but the comparison with British and German equivalents shows that it has a clear benefit in terms of responsiveness to local needs. The fragmentation of the system hinders top–down marketization initiatives from the French central state, with the beneficial results of strong local control, professional autonomy of staff and a focus on empowering clients rather than punishing them.

Members of the local networks in Seine-Saint-Denis we met were skeptical of profiteering, something they had in common with the German public employment service. Our initial approach to the field was via a multinational firm that had won a contract to deliver an experimental program for young people deemed hard to reach by the public employment service. This company advised clients in an out-of-the-way suburb. When we appeared for our second interview, the building looked like it had been shuttered. We were assured by our hosts that, although their contract had ended, the company was (like its former clients) continuing to look for work. Managers saw the end of the contract as evidence of bias against for-profit multinationals. Local officials told us that the programme had been discontinued because of poor performance.[4]

Moreover, front-line workers in French non-profit organizations were less 'disciplined' by market imperatives. In interviews, they tended to demonstrate a professional social service ethos which militated against strict conditionality and emphasized the quality of service rather than simply the volume of people finding jobs. They appeared to be genuine believers in finding sustainable jobs for their clients. They had more discretion to decide how often and for how long to see clients, as well as which services to direct them towards. They often explicitly rejected the idea of quickly 'inserting' clients into just any employment, but instead sought to locate permanent jobs where they become eligible for social insurance. The programmes they were delivering were voluntary and their clients were either outside the benefits system or receiving the safety-net benefit RSA, which was not subject (at least not in Seine-Saint-Denis) to work requirements underpinned by sanctions. While our British interviewees bemoaned the inadequate support they were able to give (or described their efforts to crack down on the workshy), our French interviewees were true believers in their approach to empowering service users (see also Fretel, 2013).

The processes at these service providers were much slower than equivalents in Britain or Germany. Assessments might take two days rather than half an hour. This would identify the work-ready to send them on job placements, and workers did refer to *écrémage*

---

[4] On the tendency of UK policymakers to disregard negative evaluation evidence for ideological reasons, see Davies (2008).

(creaming) of clients in this sense. The aim and effect, however, was not to 'park' people who were far from the labour market. It was what sociologist Serge Paugam (2002), an observer of this system at work in its early stages in the 1990s, calls sorting both for employability and for opportunity – the opportunity to take part in an intervention such as a training programme. Staff were very clear that it was important to take time, because identifying and addressing barriers to work was by its nature a task that did not lend itself to being sped up. Staff resented spending time filling in online firms – apparently a universal problem for front-line workers in employment services – but these were used to generate reports to the funder and not to manage their performance.

In Slovenia, we encountered additional problems in a study with Barbara Samaluk, now at the University of Ljubljana. We found that the destructive effects of marketization had been driven most strongly from the European level. Many Slovenian services were supported by the European Social Fund (ESF), which was increasingly tied to market-oriented conditions. As in many other new EU member states, the government was not prepared to create the commissioning procedures which were required by ESF funding conditionality. Domestic spending was decreasing and services were increasingly dependent on ESF money, meaning that these markets were not particularly lucrative or attractive to for-profit firms (Samaluk, 2017). The shift in services towards social entrepreneurship and activation introduced new ways of working that were foreign to the long-established network of small non-profits in Slovenian social services. Tenders had to be continually reissued because of a lack of appropriate providers, a process that inflicted collateral damage. It caused established career pathways for new social workers to wither away, because the organizations that would house them became much more weakly embedded and transient. Thus, it also rendered their working lives more insecure, deskilling them and reducing their professional autonomy as new bureaucratic targets came in. It also led to cuts in widely respected services in favour of contracts for unknown new players in the market (Greer et al., 2019).

The least marketized employment services were the most responsive to client needs. This is not mere correlation but reflected the priorities and strategies of government funders and the real presssures put on front-line workers and their managers. Competition on the basis of price and quality was used to re-engineer services, ensuring tight top-down control by multinational corporations (Britain) or the national public employment service (Germany). In Seine-Saint-Denis, by contrast, local networks of professionals and policymakers controlled services and governed them according to a professional ethos. In line with the occupational ethos of social workers, the desired outcome was not defined in terms of numbers of sustained job placements but rather in terms of a job with a permanent contract or a referral to an intervention led by social workers to bring clients closer to a non-precarious job placement. Thus, there was a dual process of class discipline – on service users, and the front-line workers delivering these services – which was less severe in France due to the comparative weakness of marketization there.

Offers you can't refuse?

Many unemployed workers could use assistance as they make their way in the labour market. In the wake of the Coronavirus pandemic, employment services are as necessary as ever, as large numbers of jobless people make their transitions back into the world of paid work. Unfortunately, marketized schemes are governed in ways that normally shift power away from front-line workers and local policymakers and siphons resources into commissioning bureaucracy and corporate profits. From the perspective of unemployed workers, they are also embedded in a policy of compulsion and sanctioning that can push them further to the margins of society and the labour market. This makes the working lives of front-line workers precarious and makes it difficult for them to meet the needs of their clients.

Active labour-market schemes can lubricate competition in low-wage labour markets. In their punitive form they are a class disciplinary measure, explicitly geared towards lowering the discretion of jobless workers over which jobs to apply for and take, forcing them to reduce expectations about the quality of work. But this form of marketized class discipline is implemented through another form of class discipline over employment service providers. The comparison between *insertion sociale* in Seine-Saint-Denis and workfarism in the UK makes this clear. Front-line workers in the UK had their status much reduced: it was no longer a professional social service role where the worker exercised discretion over the ways in which they interacted with clients. Instead, they had to pursue tight targets and automated systems which stripped away this autonomy. Meanwhile, their employers were insulated from this discipline by long-lasting 'black box' contracts that encouraged profit-making.

It remains to be seen how, in the wake of coronavirus, benefits systems will develop. At the height of the pandemic, work requirements were been suspended in many countries to facilitate social distancing. Where they remained, administrative chaos and political expediency often combined to make them unenforceable. It is difficult to say how much loosening there has been in sanctioning and conditionality or, where it has been loosened, how quickly they are being tightened again. Even setting aside Covid, many front-line workers believe that strict enforcement of job search rules is counterproductive in helping a client find a suitable job.

Similarly, the dilemmas that marketization of services generate do not have good solutions. For example, in employment services, reduced spending almost automatically translates into worse outcomes. During the Covid-19 era, the perceived 'danger' of rising wages in key sectors, as noted in the previous chapter, may be one factor encouraging the persistence of marketization and workfare in the coming years: the desire for class discipline may become more urgent still. The UK's relatively generous and popular furlough scheme was time-limited, and the UK government ended its sanctions moratorium in summer 2021, with monthly sanction levels quickly reaching pre-pandemic levels (Webster, 2021).

Our prediction is that dual marketization will continue past the Covid era. Whether it will ever succeed as a policy (i.e. whether it will prove itself to be an effective means of getting people into sustainable employment) is doubtful, but it appears to work well politically, and it is accelerated by the macro-level trends acting on the state which we identified in Chapter 3. In Germany, the main barrier to sanctions has not been elected politicians, but rather the constitutional court, which in 2019 forced the government to back down in sanctioning policies. This of course does not affect competitive tendering or vouchers in employment services. In Britain, where governments do not face such oversight, the government is ramping up sanctions while the pandemic continues to rage. This gives government ministers a way to show they are business-friendly, and it divides and disciplines workers, using not only a means test but also a set of increasingly sophisticated mechanisms for social control (see also Coderre-LaPalme et al., 2021).

5

The cost of healthcare marketization

In this chapter, we look at marketization in another public service, healthcare. Policymakers around Europe have worked for decades now to create 'open markets' for health services, to create a 'level playing field' between the public and private sectors and to make the public sector more 'entrepreneurial'. Things have not always gone to plan. A closer look at market mechanisms in operation reveals a chaotic picture of managers stymied in their efforts to realize profits and of activists – often successfully – struggling against policymakers' ongoing efforts to introduce them in healthcare. Marketizers have sought to avoid 'noisy' politics in reforming healthcare systems, confining their activities to the 'quiet' politics of process change and rule-making. However, they have often failed in their attempts to depoliticize healthcare, with the consequence that the expansion of for-profit healthcare has progressed more slowly than many marketizers have hoped and most opponents feared. But the intensification of competition has nonetheless affected the quality of services and jobs on the front line.

Consider the Health and Social Care Act of 2012, an attempt by a conservative-led coalition government to increase private-sector participation in England's healthcare market (it does not cover Wales, Scotland or Northern Ireland.) Despite efforts since the 1980s to make the National Health Service (NHS) more responsive and efficient through an internal market, the UK remains arguably the most state-dominated system in Europe, both in terms of funding and provision. When we were launching our large research project on marketization, the 2012 Act was the latest major attempt to promote competition and private-sector involvement in England's NHS. And yet managers and campaigners we interviewed pointed to numerous attempts to privatize services that had been abandoned. Examining these processes, and comparing them to what has happened elsewhere, reveals much about the dysfunctions of marketization.

The first major public campaign to combat the implementation of the Act was to save a heavily indebted hospital in Lewisham, South London. After a large-scale mobilization of workers and service users, the government's plan to close the hospital and restructure services was blocked in court. In 2014–15 attempts to privatize services were met with campaigns, including mental health services in Bristol, musculoskeletal services in West Sussex, management of the general hospital in Weston, adult care in Cambridgeshire, pathology in Dorset, cancer services in Staffordshire and general hospital management in Weston and Nuneaton (Coderre-LaPalme, 2018). During the 2015 general election, these campaigns were supported by Labour Party candidates for parliament, who placed defending the NHS at the centre of their campaign, and all of these privatization initiatives eventually collapsed.

For the advocates of healthcare markets, politicization is a problem. For quasi-market theorists like Julian Le Grand (2003), NHS-style health systems had the classic problems of bureaucratic socialism: services were inefficient and unresponsive to the individual needs of patients. Because a market did not yet exist, and services were public, the government would have to create a quasi-market. The key factor would be a purchasing agent that in its role as funder of services encouraged participation by diverse for-profit, non-profit and public-sector providers and determined the incentives and rules that would make them most efficient and responsive. One purpose of introducing this market-making bureaucracy is to change the incentives facing front-line workers, so that they work towards the objectives set down by marketizers rather than their other potentially conflicting professional objectives.

In healthcare, however, it is difficult to shield markets from politics. In Britain this was a constant refrain of managers in privatized health services explaining their difficulties in translating the market openings of the 2012 Act into profitable business (Krachler and Greer, 2015). In Finland's somewhat more privatized system, a conservative coalition government was voted out of office in 2019 after campaigning for a 'Sote Reform', which would have shifted responsibility for health to new regional authorities and given government-funded patients more freedom to choose for-profit and non-profit providers. In France, whose system is one of the most privatized in Europe, there were battles over how prices should be set and services planned, which often left for-profit hospitals feeling aggrieved at the 'Jacobin' French public sector. In Germany, the only country where we observed the privatization of entire local hospital systems (the largest were in the municipal hospitals of Hamburg and the university hospital Marburg-Gießen) each privatization initiative was countered by street protests and other tactics, and in a few cases campaigners managed to block privatization (Auffenberg, 2021).

These examples all illuminate how marketizers are frustrated by widespread public attention to the delivery of health services. Privatization and cuts are, in other words, politically salient, and cannot easily be done quietly. This politicization does not only concern the quality, availability or responsiveness of services. It is also about the sizeable healthcare workforce. Healthcare workers have a strong professional ethos and sense of purpose in their work, which often clashes with the logic of marketization. Health professionals are in most countries more organized into unions and professional associations than other occupations. Moreover, hospitals are among the largest employers in any city or town. In Britain and France, we documented with Genevieve Coderre-Lapalme efforts by trade unionists to counter the effects of marketization in the workplace (which we describe later in this chapter). We found that, in the wake of marketization initiatives, health workers had been mobilized to protest and strike, often for the first time, by perceived threats to the 'meaning' of healthcare work (Umney and Coderre-LaPalme, 2017). In other words, the question of how, and why, health workers do what they do.

International surveys show that public-sector healthcare enjoys overwhelming public support. The 2016 International Social Survey Programme asked citizens in thirty-nine jurisdictions, 'Do you think it should be or should not be the government's responsibility to provide health care for the sick?' In twenty-nine of these at least 95 per cent of respondents said that it 'probably' or 'definitely' should be, and in only three was it below 90 per cent (the United States, Japan and South Korea). This support has been stable since the 1980s (Coderre-LaPalme et al., 2020). Hospitals provide particularly potent symbols of accessible health services in most cities. It is therefore not surprising that, without seeking them out, from Lewisham to Hamburg, we encountered mobilizations against the restructuring of healthcare provision that followed from marketization – or that left-of-centre politicians across Europe so often place the defence of public-sector health at the centre of their messages to voters.

As far as we know, quasi-markets theorists have never tackled the question of why their proposals for healthcare are so unpopular. But beyond public opposition, two additional problems face marketizers: the additional costs incurred by creating these markets and market incentives that undermine services rather than increasing responsiveness to needs.

Consider the trend towards 'Diagnosis Related Groups' (DRGs) payments as a means of financing hospitals. This is where instead of government covering the costs hospitals have accrued in providing care, each procedure or treatment is associated with a price, usually determined beforehand, pegged to an average cost calculation made centrally. The hospital then receives funding at that rate for each of those procedures they complete (so they report to public funders not what their total costs were but how many of x procedures they did). This is intended to incentivize hospitals to minimize the costs of carrying out procedures. If the hospital can do many procedures in a cost-effective way, management can realize a surplus that can be reinvested or distributed to shareholders.

DRGs are a powerful market mechanism. Ostensibly, it is hard to compare the work that hospitals do, since the provision of healthcare has so many contingencies. Consider a homeless person or an older person who may have all sorts of interlocking chronic conditions and other life circumstances which affect the way they need to be treated and which also influence the likely results of that treatment. Or indeed anyone with either underlying conditions or comparatively precarious living conditions, or both. Treating people in these circumstances is more complex and time-consuming, with more scope for difficulties in recovery, than administering the 'same' procedure to a young, able-bodied person who has all the support she needs at home. But DRGs enable a standardized metric by which hospitals can be compared and, hence, creates the grounds for competition between them. It also involves the creation of a standardized and transparent set of rules for determining hospital budgets, thus (a marketizer might imagine) insulating the question of hospital funding from politics. With prices set before the procedure commences, the resources a hospital receives for it is no longer open for public debate, as it is a function of an objective and universally applied set of rules and calculations.

However, the implementation of DRG systems is itself a highly centralized and often expensive process, with potentially serious unanticipated consequences for services. To make them work, governments have to create detailed price lists that take into account average costs of providing different treatments. It's not a matter of 'freeing' the dynamism of competition from government bureaucracy: market competition only exists because it is enacted by government bureaucracy. But DRGs also create perverse incentives which raise costs in unanticipated ways. For instance, they provide strong incentives for providers to claim reimbursements for particularly lucrative treatments, which means providing more of these (compared to less-lucrative treatments) and making sure that procedures are coded to maximize reimbursements (also known as 'upcoding'). DRGs are just one of a dozen market mechanisms that we identified, each with a unique way of siphoning resources out of front-line services (Krachler et al., 2021). Later in this chapter, we will recount these dysfunctions and instances of profiteering in more detail.

Why do policymakers continue to pursue marketization and privatization? Part of the story is that they believe in the promises of quasi-markets for more responsive and efficient services and principles of marketization. Generation after generation of true believers can claim that healthcare has yet to harness the power of the market and point to the difference between the neoliberal ideal and the reality of their health system (Friedman, 2001).

But another reason marketization has been able to continue is that much health policy is not very politicized. The examples of politicization, we identified earlier, emerge when market mechanisms lead to privatizations and closures. When this happens, people protest in the streets, and journalists and politicians take notice. Under these conditions, business lobbyists and marketizers are less likely to prevail. But such cases are often only visible manifestations of deeper shifts that go on with little democratic scrutiny, and in fact which are purposefully shielded from it, such as changing processes for determining hospital funding and other aspects of market-making bureaucracy. Andrew Morton has uncovered an example of this in his research on the role of EU institutions, especially the Court of Justice of the EU, in determining the applicability of competition law in health systems, even though for political reasons health is ostensibly exempt (Morton, 2021). In these cases of quiet politics, marketization is unlikely to encounter as much opposition as the privatization of local services. Nonetheless, the consequences of changes made 'quietly' have serious ramifications for healthcare, including the nature of front-line work.

In the rest of this chapter, we discuss marketization in theory and practice, its consequences for work and workers, and the close but complex relationship between marketization and austerity in health.

Market principles and mechanisms

In health, as in employment services, it is important to say what exactly competition means. In our five-country study with Nick Krachler, we found that marketizers are promoting three main principles in healthcare: (1) the market should be open to diverse providers and funders; (2) there should be meaningful competition (instead of a fixed division of labour) between public and private sectors and (3) that public-sector managers should have autonomy as they compete in this market. While these market principles seem like simple statements of neoliberal common sense, the concrete mechanisms through which they are implemented are even more complex than those in employment services.

Health systems have been 'opened', for example, in three main ways. First, governments can shift funding from public to private sources, such as for-profit insurance companies or out-of-pocket spending by patients. Second, governments can financialize healthcare by using private capital to build healthcare infrastructure, particularly new hospital construction. The pre-eminent example here is Britain's Public-Private Partnerships (PPPs) or Public Finance Initiatives (PFIs). (A related trend is for private equity investors to take over already privatized services, such as occupational health in Finland and private practices in Germany.) Third, they have tried to encourage new kinds of organizations to provide healthcare services directly. This could involve selling facilities to private chains or inviting private organizations to provide additional services alongside existing public organizations.

However, opening the market does not necessarily lead to less state intervention; in fact, it can lead to significant increases in costs and bureaucratic complexity. At the time of our interviews, PFIs and PPPs in the UK were thought to be costing two billion pounds per annum more than the traditional methods of borrowing. Experiments in France and Greece with similar schemes were seen as expensive failures. But while very few interviewees had a good word to say about PFI schemes, this was not the case with other forms of 'openness'. For instance, it was not unusual to find respondents talking positively, albeit in limited and specific ways, about cases where new organizations were serving particular market niches. One European Commission official we met, who was working on healthcare and patients' rights, was particularly enthusiastic about dentists in the Czech Republic servicing patients living nearby in Germany and Austria.

Openings for new providers of services or sources of financing, however, might lead to intensified competition in theory but not in practice. Private insurers and healthcare providers find particular market niches that are profitable and that they can dominate such as elective surgeries in Britain, occupational health in Finland and exclusive hospitals and insurance for the wealthy in most countries. The public sector is left with the bulk of the population, which tends to have more and harder-to-treat health problems.

In many countries, this division of labour between public and private health providers is settled, but marketizers have increasingly sought to disrupt it, encouraging new providers to service new population groups. Marketizers have sought to level the competitive playing field through changes to payment systems or purchasing; by allowing existing public-sector providers to fail if they operate 'inefficiently'; by expanding frameworks for performance management and evaluation; by increasing patient choice; and by requiring competitive tendering for tax-funded health services. On the political left, it is often argued that politicians have acted bluntly to protect private profit, or that the system is shaped by the interests of private monopolies. But it is more complex than this. Market principles have been repeatedly adopted as an end in themselves, and new bureaucratic instruments have been laboriously developed to further that end, often with results that dissatisfy corporate elites.

The full complexity of market mechanisms is evident when working through all the mechanisms to stimulate greater competition between public and private healthcare providers.

First, consider the DRG pricing mechanisms introduced previously. France and Germany have implemented them decisively – in France, DRGs account for almost 100 per cent of hospital budgets (though the Macron government has raised the prospect of dialling this back in future), and in Germany before a 2018 reform they set payments in theory to cover all the costs of running services (investments are allegedly covered through planning by the states [*Länder*]). In both countries, price-setting policies have been complex. In the 1980s, French healthcare administrators began keeping a standardized record of procedures with associated costs, initially as a means of tracking and describing the workload of individual organizations. The prospect of using this list to finance hospitals and create incentives for them to become more efficient was only introduced much later under the Sarkozy presidency. While developing a price list for hospital services across a whole country is difficult enough, it was rendered more complex still by the unavoidable facts of hospital work: some patients are much more difficult to treat than others, even if they ostensibly have the same conditions. For instance, a homeless person requiring a surgical procedure is more costly to care for because provisions for aftercare are so much more labour-intensive than most.

The central government was therefore compelled to multiply the list of procedures and conditions in order that each one might include different entries reflecting differing degrees of severity. Complicated situations on the ground in local hospitals have been recycled into a highly centralized form of 'nuance' in the DRG list. The link between DRGs and privatization itself is unclear in France. DRGs haven't led straightforwardly to more privatization of French hospitals. In some cases, they have led to public institutions turning patients around faster, frustrating private providers who have based their model on recruiting patients from public waiting lists (while other public hospitals have been put deep into debt by the financing changes). However, in Germany it is quite direct: the new price mechanism led to resource scarcity at public hospitals, forcing restructuring. As we will show further, some *Länder* and municipalities saw privatization as an attractive solution.

DRGs are the most important market mechanisms in insurance-funded systems, because there is more scope for providers to compete against each other to attract patients. In more state-dominated systems like Britain's, changes to public purchasing make a bigger difference. Competitive tendering, for example, was the central tool used in the 2012 Act to open England's healthcare market to more private-sector providers. The same law created new bodies called 'Clinical Commissioning Groups' to purchase services from 'any qualified provider'. In principle, the NHS would have to compete with private companies for contracts. This would be achieved by allowing existing providers to fail, expanding frameworks for performance management and evaluation, increasing patient choice, and competitive tendering. While the new bodies handled purchasing at the local level, larger privatization initiatives could be carried out by regional consortia or at the national level led by NHS England.

Beyond DRGs and competitive tendering, the competitive playing field could be evened out in other ways. Under a 'failure regime', financially troubled public providers could be allowed to go out of business, instead of automatically receiving a bailout. This was what happened in the aforementioned Lewisham case, as well as in public-sector German hospitals given a private legal form. In both cases, hospitals that do not cut their costs can be shut down. Another option would be for patients to be given more choice in choosing providers, as when Finnish municipalities issued vouchers to pay for services in cases where much-needed public provision was scarce, and in the efforts of the European Commission to require health insurance to pay for patients who cross national borders for treatment.

A final market principle in healthcare is that public-sector managers should be given more autonomy to compete. Giving public hospitals a private legal form, as with foundation trusts in England or municipally owned corporations (with the private legal form GmbH) in Germany, is one way to unshackle management to compete on the market. The development of internal markets has required individual public organizations to compete via tenders to be assigned work, suggesting a further multiplication of tendering and commissioning procedures, in order to stimulate competition between public managers within different organizations. In the NHS, this has also involved new centrally dictated incentive schemes. For instance, the institution of Foundation Trust status for public-sector hospitals was intended to incentivize improved performance with centrally defined levels or tiers. This led to the proliferation of indicators, targets and benchmarks to facilitate the assessments needed to allow trusts to climb up the hierarchy.

Another way to make public-sector organizations more autonomous is decentralizing regulation. The creation of regional health agencies in France, for example, was supposed to give regulators greater autonomy to plan healthcare provision in a more responsive way to local needs. This is an important point, because it enables us to identify another rationale for marketization: responsiveness to the bespoke needs of local populations which are presumed to be impossible for 'monolithic' central public-sector organizations. But as we will see, empirically it doesn't necessarily work out like this.

All of this underlines that in healthcare, marketization does not mean 'less government': it is government that introduces market mechanisms, and government agencies play an important role in service provision, funding and regulation. Opening the market, creating a level competitive playing field and freeing public-sector providers to compete are easier said than done, and the mechanisms to implement these principles are complex. This complexity provides some cover for marketizers, but not often enough to avoid conflict with workers and citizens.

Class discipline and pushback

It would be fanciful to explain healthcare marketization as a simple consequence of efforts to reduce bureaucracy and maximize cost-effectiveness. Through more than 100 interviews across five countries, we spoke to managers, trade unionists, politicians and private-sector healthcare managers and lobbyists. It became apparent that the negative stories they had to tell about marketization tended to outweigh the positive ones, not just in terms of service quality but also in terms of cost. We unpack some of this in the remaining sections of this chapter, emphasizing our central themes of the disciplining of workers and the subversion of democratic oversight.

The effects of marketization on healthcare work have been profound, and in various respects, market mechanisms have exerted a disciplinary impetus on front-line workers. But because some medical practitioners have also benefitted, our analysis needs to tread carefully. To contextualize, we can start by observing a long-running tension in healthcare work between professional notions of care and the imperatives of the economic systems in which healthcare is embedded. Medical practitioners on the left have often argued for a more holistic view of medicine, where the practitioner pays close attention to the social situation of patients and views disease not as a discrete problem to be solved through a specific procedure, but as closely shaped by social structures[1]. In light of the current Covid-19 pandemic, we can easily see the validity of this argument, given that many aspects of the way our societies are organized have shaped the trajectory of the disease. Consider how the demands of 'the economy' and the lack of paid leave for many workers have encouraged people to attend work and thus spread the virus, or the way in which specific institutions like care homes and universities have become vectors of transmission.

This more holistic approach contrasts with medical practice as it has evolved, which has tended to favour increasing specialization as medicine becomes more advanced. As a market for medical services developed, individual practitioners and providers became increasingly associated with particular, discrete functions. The profit motive is also important context here, because in a liberal medical system it may be that medical practitioners, required to specialize, will choose to do so in disciplines which enable the best living to be made rather than those which are most needed in communities. Part of the socialist critique of medicine in capitalist societies is that the public (or state) renounces much control over the supply side (see Chandra and Chandra, 2020), leading to gaps in underserved (or unprofitable) aspects of medical practice.

---

[1] These comments are indebted to Chandra and Chandra (2020).

This idea of a holistic versus market-oriented medical practice resurfaced frequently during our interviews in various different guises. Indeed, it was becoming particularly salient in the wake of the introduction of market mechanisms, as we will show momentarily. We see the increasing fragmentation of healthcare work as in some cases leading to class discipline. This, of course, requires qualification. Medical practitioners, particularly those that successfully carve out lucrative niches, can benefit hugely from market-facing specialization: indeed, for them it may be empowerment, not discipline.

But this is not the whole story. Our interviews with hospital staff revealed that for many, marketization had indeed unleashed disciplinary pressures and a more oppressive version of specialization. Interviewees told us about numerous instances where the agency and autonomy of workers to do their jobs as they see fit was weakened, as was their ability to negotiate or dispute the rules set down by managers and government. For many medical practitioners, these pressures can be compensated by the benefits of providing specialized medical services privately. So our aim here is not to paint a simple picture of the proletarianization of medical practice. Marketization leads to class discipline in healthcare often in subtle ways, but which produce controversies around the meaning and ethos of healthcare practice and the prerogatives of the people who do it.

There were many occasions where market mechanisms had led to workers feeling forced to make what they felt were bad decisions that were not in patients' best interest or did not correspond to their understandings of professional practice. For example, by creating strong incentives to reduce the cost of treating each diagnosis, DRG systems led to the speeding up of healthcare work. Hospitals would lose money if patients stayed longer than absolutely necessary. The rhythms of work thus became increasingly determined by government funding systems rather than healthcare workers themselves. Interviewees complained that this meant they had to abandon aspects of the job they had previously seen as vital, such as spending time talking with patients, to understand their situation not just clinically but socially (since patient's social environment and living arrangements can have a material effect on the progression or recovery from illness).

Furthermore, many noted that the logic of DRGs had enforced the logic of specialization, encouraging healthcare providers to abandon services that were less 'profitable' under DRGs. For instance, one French interviewee recounted how his hospital had previously offered certain free services (such as eye tests) to homeless people in their city who did not have insurance to cover it. But following the switch to DRG funding they had had to abandon this. Why? Because the hospital typically served patients who took longer to treat and required more support. These issues were not recognized in the DRG standardized valuations, even after the degrees of severity were brought in. As such, the new price structure threw the hospital into deficit overnight, forcing it to abandon discretionary services to meet real medical and social needs. Hence, we have a contradictory and tension-laden dynamic: opportunities for lucrative specialization for some, proceeding in tandem with a stripping away of more holistic and discretionary aspects of the job. Note that this can also cost more money in the long run, interviewees claimed, because patients' conditions get worse and become harder because they weren't dealt with properly the first time (what some French respondents called *le patient boomerang*).

This line of argument was also connected to one of the common complaints about competitive tendering. Private-sector actors who were looking to provide services tended to specialize in particular low-acuity conditions, because they could be performed relatively profitably. The desire to increase public-private competition via tendering systems was thus locked into a mutually reinforcing dynamic with the breaking up of medical practice into discrete and specialized tasks. Combine this with increased cost pressures and management given greater discretion to respond to them, and we can start to see a convergence of pressures on many hospital workers where defined procedures and targets are imposed which sit in tension with professional discretion and agency.

Indeed, privatization has been a vital tool of class discipline in many cases. In England's health service following the 2012 Act, private providers sought to further their integration into the system by undercutting existing NHS providers, and a key means of doing this was sweating their workers in ways that were not possible in the NHS. This has included employing lower-skilled workers to do tasks that require higher qualifications in the NHS, avoiding collective bargaining, using techniques of 'intensive asset utilization' to sweat physical assets, and standardizing performance management techniques to speed up work (Krachler and Greer, 2015).

Likewise in German hospitals, privatizations had similar disciplinary effects, notably by forcing hospital staff to accelerate their work, but also through a pay squeeze. The extension of private hospital care had led to decreases in the number of nursing, technical and other staff grades (not including doctors) alongside increases in patient numbers. While this was seen by advocates of marketization as potentially positive (supposedly signifying a cheaper but faster system of care), once again the discretion of hospital workers was reduced, as was time spent with patients that could not be reimbursed under the pricing system. At the same time, hospital workers' ability to influence their conditions of work also weakened, because the fragmentation of the system through privatization and outsourcing of services led to the breakup of the collective bargaining system, and therefore divergences in the terms and conditions of work by function and firm (Greer et al., 2013).

This last point indicates how marketization also corroded the voice mechanisms of medical professionals in the way their facilities were organized. In French public hospitals, for instance, the internal organization of hospitals had been reworked. Governance committees which had previously involved a stronger voice for represented members of both medical and technical staff were being downgraded, and decision-making power was being concentrated in the hands of the hospital directorate, who in turn was directly hired and fired by public authorities. This stripping out of voice within the hospital workplace had emerged to increase the responsiveness of hospital managers to market pressure. When we talk about decentralization, therefore, there is a big difference between the decentralization which empowers medical staff on the ground, and the 'decentralization' which allows hospital managers to respond more rapidly to cues set by a (centrally organized) market.

Interestingly, then, but perhaps unsurprisingly, we saw changes in the way workers' representatives were responding to the situation. In particular, we started to observe unions campaigning more explicitly around the meaning of work. A French trade unionist said,

> We consider that we are not *producteurs du soin* ('manufacturers of care'). The logic is that the hospital is a business producing health care. We say that it doesn't work like that. The taking care of patients is very complex. It's not just technique, and the more the population ages, the less it's about technique. . . . It's time, it's words- when we reassure the person and explain their illness, or explain their treatment. . . . Because that time, in the *chemin productiviste* ('productivist pathway') that we face today, that doesn't exist. It considers it as time lost. . . . So what we trade unionists are demanding now is: return the meaning to work. Work in teams . . . and above all, value human relationships with patients . . . Voila. Today, people are worn out. They no longer find meaning in their work. (Umney and Coderre-LaPalme, 2017)

Likewise in the UK, previously non-militant professional associations such as certain Royal Colleges (notably the Royal College of Midwifery which went on strike for the first time in 2014), were moved to a more militant posture by the belief that professional status was being undermined by the 2012 Act. Marketization thus succeeded, to a degree, in riling up various sections of the previously comparatively nonconfrontational healthcare workforces (Umney and Coderre-LaPalme, 2017).

Marketization of healthcare systems also creates new processes and institutions which obstruct public scrutiny and democratic oversight. Indeed, this is partially the point of innovations like DRG systems and elaborate criteria for competitive tendering: they impose a 'transparent' system for allocating resources which resists political interference. The consequences of DRGs in health services, however, are in fact prone to dysfunctions and pushback, as we have seen. Marketization has not simply erased democratic oversight in health systems. It has engendered recurrent and sometimes paralysing tensions between the centralizing thrust of marketization and pushback against this by health workers, the public and even within public bureaucracies themselves, where people are concerned about their effects.

Marketization also enables the state to wash its hands of some responsibilities in providing care, which causes problems for wider populations. Cost-shifting, for instance, is when individuals are required to top up public support with additional privately purchased insurance or out-of-pocket spending. This increases healthcare costs to individuals, and increases the risk that they will forgo treatment they need because of the expense. This removes responsibility from the state for providing certain services and makes inadequacies of provision into a private problem for individuals to solve, rather than a public issue. Similarly, when work is privatized, the management of the system is shifted from a public administration issue to a private-sector management problem. In sum, various health systems have used particular forms of marketization to reduce the responsibilities of public authorities and individualize responsibility for health coverage, which has produced problems of diminishing health coverage.

We also need to note some of the institutional dysfunctions created by market mechanisms, which further undermine coherent political oversight within health systems. In France, for instance, we observed the tensions embedded in the role of the *Agences Régionales de Santé* (ARS) institutions. These regional public authorities were created in 2010, ostensibly with extensive powers to intervene in local health systems to tailor them to local needs. They didn't have an electoral mandate, and their leadership was appointed from the centre. They could, theoretically, compel providers of services, be they public or private, to work together to deliver certain functions. And indeed, in doing so they were supposed to be able to transcend the established public-private division of labour in their territories, bringing everyone together into a shared set of objectives. From this perspective, they are not necessarily highly marketized institutions. They are supposed to be planning institutions with the power to shape healthcare in a way that is not beholden to market competition and which has a more holistic view of local service provision (Umney and Coderre-LaPalme, 2021).

But this vision of local planning was fundamentally in conflict with other ongoing trends in French health policy. First, central austerity imperatives from the French government meant the ARSes became bogged down in controversial and politicized process of shutting down local supply. They were forced to become the 'armed wing' of the state in overseeing local closures. But in addition to this, local agency found itself in conflict with the centralized strictures imposed by marketization. Interviewees argued that the ARSes had little power to institute new forms of supply and cooperation, because their initiatives were undermined by the centrally dictated DRG system. The latter imposed a set of priorities from above that encouraged hospitals to accelerate their own processes and disincentivized collaboration. One academic interviewee said many hospital managers had responded to the DRG system with a 'bad attitude', but a private hospital manager merely noted that there was little point cooperating with other local providers, since their budget depended exclusively on the hospital completing as many reimbursable procedures as it could.

While ARSes had had their own sources of additional discretionary funding, these were very small and in practice the state tried to overrule them when they took an excessively qualitative view on how to award them (Guerrero et al., 2009). Ultimately, then, marketization had constrained the ability of local actors to take control over the planning of healthcare provision. Indeed, Gerard Vincent (2012), an observer of French hospital policy, notes that one purpose of the DRG pricing system was to stop regional actors developing their own bespoke funding systems. Combine this with the increasing centralization of power within hospitals themselves, and it's clear that marketization has been a centralizing process which has squeezed out scope for 'political' input from workers and citizens within the system.

The politics of privatization, quiet and noisy

One of the puzzling features of health marketization is that no side of the debate is satisfied: How can it be that trade unionists and healthcare campaigners say the principles of health systems are under attack from privatization and competition, while managers of for-profit enterprises still bemoan the barriers to doing business? Untangling these tensions requires us to understand the difference between the quiet and noisy forms of politics that accompany marketization.

The campaign against the closure of Lewisham was important but by no means unusual for Britain or other countries, as we showed previously, nor was it new for Britain (Ruane, 2011). This is an example of a situation where the consequences of marketization are brought out into the open, and where campaigners can use the 'noisy' politics of protest to successfully fight marketization. Marketizers, therefore, tend to complain about noisy politics.

But vital aspects of marketization can also be quiet and technocratic, and these are the kinds that are often hardest to oppose. We first encountered this problem when talking with German trade unionists in 2003 about their attempts to shape the 2002 reforms that introduced a DRG pricing system for medical procedures. While they knew that a more competitive healthcare market would be a threat to public hospitals, their efforts to mount a campaign were stifled by the highly technocratic nature of the issues involved and the well-organized business interests (most notably insurers and private GPs) that dominated the discussions. Their proposals were accepted in 'homeopathic doses'. Furthermore, concepts such as DRGs often have a deceptively simple logic to them, creating a misleading sense of transparency and procedural legitimacy which appears to resist politicization. This can also be a problem in the NHS: campaigners report that it is hard work to explain the mechanics of commissioning and the processes through which it can lead to privatization.

In NHS-style systems like Britain and Finland, the central government can be held accountable for decisions over both funding and provision. Decisions over funding in these systems are closely related to decisions over provision, and when governments make changes to funding, it soon becomes apparent to campaigners that this also has important implications for provision. And this can lead to effective and noisy protest initiatives. In Britain, this took the form of a series of campaigns against local privatization initiatives by the local Clinical Commissioning Groups (CCGs) created by the 2012 Act, and in Finland it took the form of a general election campaign that ousted a government planning marketization. In these countries, public funding for public providers is regularly tweaked to cover their running costs.

In insurance-funded systems, by contrast, the quiet politics of marketization are separate from the noisy politics of privatization, and this has made campaigning against marketization more difficult. In Germany, for example, where we examined some very large cases of privatization, the proximate cause of privatization was that a state or municipal provider ran into financial trouble, in part because DRGs do not adequately cover costs, which in turn reflects how government austerity policies lead to an investment backlog. As in Lewisham, financial pressures combined with the threat of bankruptcy to produce restructuring. In each of the German cases we examined, restructuring plans met a campaign of resistance, which was often not only sophisticated and innovative but was also often ineffective.

The largest hospital privatization case was in Hamburg, the German *Land* that in 2003 privatized its Landesbetrieb Krankenhäuser. Previous centre–left governments had closed one of the hospitals, given management more autonomy through a new private legal form, and worked intensively with trade unionists to make the hospitals more efficient. A newly elected right-wing government (a coalition of conservatives, liberals and right-wing populists) moved immediately to sell the hospitals to the private firm, Asklepios. Beyond their belief that government should not be providing healthcare, this was a way for the government to wash its hands of responsibility for expected cuts to public-sector health services.

The campaign in Hamburg against privatization was innovative and multifaceted. It included trade unionists, not only the doctors' union Marburger Bund and the services union *ver.di*, but also the local umbrella body the DGB, and numerous other partners. One innovative tactic was to organize a ballot initiative against privatization, which required activists to gather tens of thousands of signatures and further cemented the work between the unions and partners. In 2004, nearly three-quarters of the electorate voted to block privatization. Because the initiative was not legally binding, however, and possibly because the Conservatives substantially increased their share of the vote in the same election, the *Land* Hamburg moved ahead with the transfer of three-quarters ownership to Asklepios. In the face of a new, even broader campaign for the *Land* to respect the lopsided vote against privatization, the new owner confirmed workers' fears through further job cuts, exit from the collective agreement, and negotiation of a concessionary agreement with *ver.di*. (Greer, 2008b). The quiet work of reshaping the incentives and financial pressures of the DRG system created a strong business case for right-wing politicians in cities and Länder to implement privatization and override objections. Their strongly institutionalized position, as elected officials with powers spelled out in a written constitution, helped them to push privatization through, even in the face of loud protests and sophisticated campaigns of resistance.

DRGs can thus serve as a potent tool for the restructuring of services while stifling or negating protest. They create a framework in which cuts are rendered necessary, regardless of ownership. These cuts need not take the form of privatization. In France, like in German municipalities governed by the centre–left, the issue is not privatization, but rather the closure of services. French private hospitals – which have a far greater market share than Finnish, German or British counterparts – have a longstanding division of labour with the public sector, serving a more upscale clientele. While DRGs were supposed to promote competition between public and private sectors, this has not happened (to the disappointment of French advocates of private healthcare that we interviewed). Instead, it has put pressures on public hospitals to increase their productivity. Protests against closing a French emergency room or privatizing a German hospital falter, because they do not address the root causes which lie in the quiet politics of marketization: complex decisions made about market rules which have been made many years before without much in the way of democratic scrutiny. Without re-politicizing these quiet changes in health policy, campaigners may not be successful on the noisier terrain of challenging their consequences.

In health, there are enough areas of relatively little public scrutiny for market openings to appear and for private firms to have some success in taking advantage of these openings. Since healthcare is a vast industry, accounting for anywhere from 5 per cent to 12 per cent of GDP in European countries (and 17 per cent in the United Sates), the opportunities for making profit are substantial, even with small increases in private-sector involvement. Where hospital privatization has been most widespread, in Germany, profiteering has been blatant and obvious. In 2013, shareholders in the Rhön Klinikum, which had taken over numerous public hospitals, received a special dividend of more than €1.9 billion, when the chain was purchased by competitor Fresenius (Burger and Gould, 2013). However, the system is politicized enough – especially when it comes to the question of private ownership – for marketizers and profiteers to experience considerable frustration.

Paying the bill

The pandemic has temporarily changed the debate over health systems, and the costs of marketization are more salient than ever before. The NHS was warned in 2014 that the redefinition of excess staff and resources as 'waste' – to be reduced by autonomized public-sector hospital management – was leaving the UK vulnerable to a pandemic (Leys, 2020). Writers on French healthcare have argued that the pandemic must prompt a rethink of DRG systems, because a system which defines unused hospital capacity as 'wastage' is sure to be left cruelly exposed under these circumstances (Grimaldi and Pierru, 2020). The trend towards closing German hospitals has continued throughout the pandemic, albeit not as rapidly as think tanks such as the Bertelsmann Stiftung have proposed (Schwager, 2021). The poor and marginalized have disproportionately paid for marketization in terms of body count: in healthcare, with the welfare state and in other areas too.

The Indian academics and activists Pratyush and Pritha Chandra (2020) argue that the central problem of capitalist medicine is the way the public has to relinquish control over supply. Questions of what kind of services are provided, by whom, to whom and where are shielded from democratic input. Under DRGs and autonomized public-sector management, this loosening of public control is quite deliberate, although in France and Germany supply is subject to regional planning by government. However, the dysfunctions of marketization sometimes call for government intervention, especially during the pandemic. French president Emmanuel Macron, who once said 'there's no magic money' for health funding during a visit to a hospital, announced during the Covid-19 crisis that 'health is priceless' (Sicot, 2020).

We cannot yet say what the long-term implications of the pandemic and its associated effects will be for healthcare marketization. We would be surprised if it led to a fundamental rethink of competition as an organizing principle, and yet the extreme pressures caused by the pandemic will force some changes. At present, health workers are winning improvements through striking, not only regarding pay and benefits but also systemic improvements that reduce their on-the-job stress, such as staffing ratios (Wills, 2021).

In the UK, for instance, the mounting backlog of people awaiting treatment, and the desire to get this down quickly, is leading to attempts to reduce the burden of commissioning and tendering, particularly in the form of the Health and Care Bill (due to become law in 2022)[2].

---

[2]   See former UK Health Secretary Matt Hancock's speech explaining the rationale for the Health and Care Bill in February 2021: *Health and Social Care Secretary Matt Hancock on Proposals for a Health and Care Bill – GOV.UK* (www.gov.uk).

In an emergency, the bureaucratic apparatus of marketization has become a severe burden: public authorities want services to be provided quickly and tendering processes following competitive rules are a hindrance. Yet it is possible that UK government attempts to prune this bureaucracy will lead to sweeter deals and less oversight for private companies (for instance, if the new Bill allows services to be awarded to companies without a tendering process). It may prove an easier route to privatization than through the ostensibly open competition organized by CCGs, and this is why it attracts much opposition. So we may see a model where the apparatus of marketization is cut back in an attempt to save time and energy, but in a manner which allows further private-sector entrenchment.[3] Indeed, one reason the UK government is seeking to strip away competitive tendering obligations may be because, as we have seen, the institutions through which they were managed were too brittle and susceptible to protest. Can privatization be done more quietly? Another interesting question is how this will divide opponents of Conservative health reforms in the UK. Numerous voices have railed against the cronyism and privatization they believe will be enabled by the Health and Care Bill, while others (like the union Unison) see it with cautious optimism as a reduction in the hold of competition law over the NHS (Gorton, 2021). Time will tell whether these changes enable a more positive alternative to marketization, a noncompetitive oligarchy, or a situation where private actors are given new powers to organize competition on their own terms.

The frustrations facing privatizers are not reasons for defenders of health systems to be complacent. In France, Germany, Britain and elsewhere, this lack of complacency among campaigners has been an important reason why health systems are so resilient. Even setting aside the damage done by partial and dysfunctional forms of marketization, we have drawn attention to another consequence of the marketization

---

[3] For a comment on the bill which emphasizes its potential to enable deeper private-sector integration into the NHS, see Molloy (2021).

agenda in healthcare: the disciplining of the health workforce. This process is inevitably limited, because workers contest it fiercely, and because healthcare simply can't function without the professionalism and discretion of front-line workers. But marketization is reshaping healthcare work in ways which are not conducive to the holistic models of practice required in a pandemic.

In the Covid pandemic, health systems are at a breaking point, in part due to the shortage of staff and capacity caused by years of marketization and economization. But there are slower-burning and more hidden issues in marketized healthcare. If private hospitals free up beds to treat Covid-19 patients and postpone anything deemed nonessential, who covers the operating loss? In insurance-funded systems, how much will governments pay to bail out financially troubled insurers and providers, and how much of the cost will they shift onto patients (in the form of higher prices) and workers (in the form of devaluing their work)? How much additional expense will governments accept to keep private providers in the marketplace?

6

Live music

Digitalization and marketization in the original gig economy

Governments that want to marketize health and welfare systems face obstacles, such as unwieldy and expensive bureaucratic processes, concerns about cost and quality, and the protests of workers and citizens. But it is not just governments who re-engineer services using price competition.

In this chapter, we look at marketization in the very different context of live music. This may seem odd, since live music seems to be the most competitive market imaginable. Aside from a small number of elite 'stars',[1] price-based competition in live music is already widespread, intense and anarchic. Anyone who has tried to earn money from live music understands these difficulties, which became much worse during the pandemic when nearly all work dried up. The number of people wanting to work exceeds the opportunities available by some distance. There is always someone willing to work for a lower fee, and formal rules about pay and conditions, whether set by government, unions or collective bargaining are often (but as we shall see, not always) dead letter.

From the perspective of a live music worker, the market is already forbiddingly competitive. Does this mean the work of marketization is already done?

---

[1] Readers interested in that market segment can consult Krueger (2019).

Not quite. In what follows, we will examine recent attempts to expand and intensify price-based competition in live music. The marketizers, in this case, are not policymakers but entrepreneurs, who attempt to make profits by intervening in the exchange process. In many cases inspired by the language of the 'platform economy' and funded by venture capitalists, new digital intermediaries have emerged which seek to make themselves indispensable by staging competition among live musicians. They would seem to have a much simpler task than policymakers engaged in marketizing health or welfare services, since they do not face government bureaucracy, political opposition or a workforce with strong unions or employment rights. But there are significant barriers to creating an Uber for live music, albeit different ones from introducing market mechanisms in health and employment services.

Live music, it transpires, is not just an interesting case of real-world marketization. It also enables the investigation of another closely related phenomenon: that of the 'platform economy' and its limits. The term, at least as it is applied to labour markets, is often used vaguely. It gestures towards a supposed new economic model where people work independently, accessing a series of one-off jobs in a 'flexible' way through digital apps (archetypal examples would be the ride-hailing company Uber or the food delivery company Deliveroo). This model has a certain affinity to marketization: compared to the so-called standard employment relationship, barriers to entry are low and transactions rapid. Presenting it as some kind of new normal for labour markets may serve a propagandistic purpose by encouraging workers to lower their expectations regarding pay and job security. However, the share of the workforce that relies on labour-based apps for paid work is small (Huws, 2021; O'Farrell and Montagnier, 2019), and investors may be growing tired of zeitgeisty but unprofitable ventures (Madrigal, 2019).

This book is less concerned with grand narratives of epochal industrial transformation and more concerned with how markets are reorganized using digital tools. Our goal is to illuminate the class discipline that digital intermediaries exercise over working musicians to realize profits.

To find this out, we need to be precise about what we mean by 'platforms', as well as the broader term 'digitalization'. The latter simply means a substantial increase in the use of digital technologies in a given situation. But a platform is more specific. It is a digital infrastructure that enables multiple parties to interact. This might include 'customers, advertisers, service providers, producers, suppliers and even physical objects' (Srnicek, 2017). On a platform, each of these is supposed to be an active participant. Uber is a platform because both passenger and driver can log on as they choose, accept rides, give ratings to each other and so on. But an online directory of taxi providers would not be a platform because only the person browsing it is active. The drivers whose contact details are listed just have to wait for people to contact them. Platforms also amass data, particularly through rating systems (where for instance you may assign another platform participant a score depending on the quality of your interaction with them). These feed into algorithms that make suggestions ('you liked x; now try y') and also enforce rules and performance norms ('your average star rating is too low; your account has been deactivated'). The more data and participants platforms amass, the better they work.

For some authors, platforms embody a kind of total marketization. They turn everyone into an individual market participant, alongside thousands of others, imposing a vicious kind of all-against-all competition in which all countervailing social protections melt away. From a Polanyian perspective, this is the main reason the platform model is likely to fail. It strips out all the social underpinnings upon which human society relies, damaging the social relations needed to coordinate production, and inevitably producing a countermovement (Fleming et al., 2019).

For us, however, this is too broad-brush. It overstates the likelihood of a social countermovement against the market, glosses over the complicated and conflictual ways in which price competition is extended in the first place and obscures the class disciplinary effects of marketization initiatives, in favour of a more nebulous focus on the preservation of society as a whole.

In live music, platforms and other digitalized market intermediaries have been created to accelerate transactions between musicians and their customers. They have typically done this by creating online spaces where thousands of musicians (as well as, in some cases, other market participants like venue owners) can be compared, ranked in terms of price and rated. To some extent, this has disciplined the live music workforce by forcing them to lower their expectations about prices and working conditions and become more attentive to competition and 'customer service'. But this marketization process has brought enterprises into conflict with other aspects of the live music industry which act as subtle brakes on the smooth running of competition. Examining it in detail tells us much about the disciplinary effects of marketization, as well as its frailties.

Marketizing in a gig economy

What does it mean to expand and intensify price-based competition, in a market where there is already so much labour oversupply that it's become increasingly normal not only to work for free but also to pay to work? (Greer et al., 2018). This is the question facing students of live music markets. To answer it, we need to know more about the dynamics of labour markets in the industry.

Live music is dominated by freelancers. Outside of major orchestras and musical theatres, live musicians rarely have an ongoing employment relationship. They transact directly with clients such as band leaders or venues, setting their own fees and deciding what to do with the proceeds they make from gigs. This doesn't mean that businesses cannot extract profits from live musicians. They just have to do it in different ways. One way is through intermediation, organizing transactions between the musician and the client. They may promise to link a client up with a given musician, or vice versa, in exchange for a fee. This is the role of the agent, a well-known and important figure throughout the history of the arts and entertainment industries. Most musicians do not have agents and getting recruited by one may be a key 'break' for artists that opens new career opportunities (Lizé et al., 2020).

Traditionally, agents tended to limit market competition to up-sell the acts they represented. Traditional agents represent a closed roster of musicians, who they might have hand-picked, and use their networks and schmoozing skills to seek out work for these select artists. They decide, as *gatekeepers*, who enters the market. By limiting which musicians can access good gigs, and by acting as a representative for those who can (negotiating better prices and working conditions), they limit the scope of price competition and greatly accentuate the importance of interpersonal social networks in deciding who gets what. In the UK, groups representing agents are involved in collective bargaining with entertainment workers' unions, which determines commission rates and other industry practices (Umney, 2017). Through much of the twentieth century, musicians in the United States and Britain would have found work through union hiring halls, where jobs are posted directly via the union, which determined rates and restricted market access to its own members in good standing, thus keeping a relatively tight control over competition (Commons, 1906). But those days are long gone.

Digital technologies would seem to threaten the traditional agent model, because they raise the possibility of much larger and more open ways of linking up musicians and clients. For example, where an internet search for live bands takes customers to sites where they can browse through thousands of available acts. By creating online 'platforms' for doing this, intermediaries may find new ways of making profits. Not by acting as selected musicians' representatives, but by providing a one-stop venue for exchange between a much larger array of buyers and sellers. The aim is to facilitate a higher volume of transactions, rendering the exchange process more expansive and user-friendly (from a buyer's perspective), and being rewarded for this through the fees they get each time a gig is arranged. The next section shows in more depth how digital intermediaries have tried to accomplish this work of marketization. It focuses on two distinct kinds of initiative: we will call the first 'digitalized agencies' and the second 'live music platforms'.

Digitalized agencies

Live music is highly fragmented. Compare (1) playing in a symphony orchestra to (2) performing original songs with your own band in a small venue or (3) playing background music in a hotel lobby or at a wedding reception. These different kinds of live music work involve different ways of doing business. They rely on different networks of venues and intermediaries. They connect with different audiences. The motivations and expectations of the musicians themselves are different and so are the informal norms around how workers should be treated, including expectations about pay. But any given individual musician may do all three of them in varying combinations in order to build up their career and income.

The kinds of marketization that occur differ between 'function' and 'original' music work. By function music, we mean music performed as an auxiliary service. These acts play a set repertoire of familiar party songs at a wedding (*Brown-Eyed Girl*, *Superstition*, etc.) or run through easy listening standards at a corporate event. Musicians are part of the service team for an event, along with catering and security staff[2]. By 'original' music, we mean cases where the musician is performing their own creative output. Obviously, this could encompass a vast array of styles and venues. We will say more about this later.

Some markets for function music are being consolidated and reorganized by digitalized intermediaries. Imagine booking a wedding band. One common way to do this would be through word of mouth, asking personal contacts with connections to the music scene. Another way would be to get in touch with an entertainment agency that will have

---

[2]   The sociologist of music work Marc Perrenoud (2006) refers to this as 'auxiliary' music work.

acts on their roster they can recommend. In either case, a huge marketplace of jobbing musicians may in theory be available, but in fact from the client's perspective options are quite limited. Only a relatively narrow range of contacts and information is available to the average buyer. If they go through word of mouth they may only have access to a couple of acts, and if they go through an agent they rely on their roster. Consequently, informal kinds of regulation, such as widely held rules of thumb around what constitutes a fair price for a band, are likely to influence the kind of deals that get made. Indeed, our research revealed that function musicians tend to have very clear and consistent ideas about going rates, and try to enforce them when they deal with clients (Umney, 2016). So, despite the near-total absence of a formal regulatory framework, market competition is limited by the lack of information in a fragmented market, making it hard to access a wide range of performers. This fragmented market is regulated by informal social norms to a surprising extent.

But this is not how many people today would book a wedding band. Instead, they might simply enter into an internet search engine something like 'book band for wedding in Leeds'. Such a search brings up digitalized intermediaries, some of them resembling traditional agents and others being online directories featuring potentially thousands of acts, which potential customers can browse and compare. On the larger sites, the customer typically uses a series of drop-down menus to specify what they are looking for: the date and location, the type of event, the type of music required, their preferred price range and so on. Then, potential customers are offered a list of acts to browse, often quite long. The information about each act may include past customer ratings and testimonials, as well as audio-visual materials such as promotional videos.

This is digitally enabled marketization. These sites attempt to consolidate a huge array of musicians (who otherwise are mainly accessible through thousands of separate word-of-mouth networks or via a gatekeeper like an agent) into an online space in which they can all be compared against each other more or less instantaneously. It creates a common set of parameters to aid the smooth running of price competition: the artists on offer display their prices up-front and can be sorted accordingly, and in some cases can be ranked by indicators such as 'popularity' (though it may be unclear how this is calculated). Compared to a traditional agent, digitalized agencies tend to be less selective about which musicians are able to make it onto their roster (normally there is a simple sign-up link and form), which further facilitates market entry, including even to very inexperienced musicians. The market is opened, and comparability is enhanced.

These sites are not 'platforms', however. They are one-sided (rather than multi-sided) markets, because the bands involved are usually passive, waiting for a prospective client to take an interest in their profile, whereupon the two parties are usually put into email contact with each other. The website may contain large amounts of information, but in our research we found that ratings were not widely used and it was difficult to compare the quality of acts with the information available (Azzellini et al., 2021). The price on the website, when available, was usually a starting point, which served as the grounds for further offline negotiations accounting for travel time, length of the concert and myriad other contingencies. The band is still usually paid directly by the client on the night, rather than via the online system.

In this example, digital tools are used to extend and intensify price competition in live music, but with the important caveat that this remains a fairly human-centric process. Levels of automation fall way short of what would be expected from an ideal-typical platform. When looking at function music, it is clear that some form of digitalization has enabled marketization. But as we will show later in this chapter, a more rapid and complete shift towards a platform model is not necessary for achieving class discipline and the extraction of profits, which from the perspective of the capitalist is fundamental.

Uber for live music?

In more 'original' or 'creative' types of music work, there are genuine platforms. One such example is Gigmit, which is based in Berlin and claims to have over 60,000 acts, and has received financial backing from Sony as well as the European Social Fund. There are various similar enterprises, which tend to have many more musicians signed up than the digitalized agencies discussed previously. This is partly because the people wanting to play original music greatly outnumber those looking for function work (since many function musicians will also be looking for opportunities to play original work, and they will be joined by many others who have day jobs outside music entirely but are looking to develop a passion project or catch a break). Furthermore, their expectations for pay are generally much lower.

These sites work differently from the digitalized agencies and conform more closely to the platform model. They are multi-sided markets because all participants are active. Musicians can post their profiles, but venues and concert organizers can create their own as well and in some cases so can other entities like record labels or studios. These parties interact with the platform; nobody is in the position of passively waiting to be contacted. A venue organizing an event might post an announcement (including details such as the fee to be paid) and individuals, bands or labels could approach the organizer; the resulting transaction would be hosted by the platform.

The volume of data used is also much greater. For instance, on various live music platforms, musicians' profiles are synced to other sites such as Youtube, Twitter and SoundCloud, supposedly as a means of amassing a more sophisticated and comprehensive dataset for judging the quality and popularity of participants – and hence for enhancing comparability. Some even feature automated discipline systems. If one participant lets down another (for instance, if a musician commits to a gig and then doesn't show up), this can be recorded and used to disconnect them from the platform if it happens multiple times.

This business model is much closer to the ideal of the platform economy than digitalized intermediaries in function music. But, what was immediately obvious when examining these sites, was that the industry is still some way from being significantly reshaped by this technology. The platforms are generally underwhelming, confined to the margins of the marketplace. The odds of getting a gig through these sites were long: one site reported advertising 2,000 gigs per year for 40,000 musicians registered, and another reported 2,000 gigs per year for nearly 60,000 musicians and DJs registered. The work on offer there tends to be very low quality, such as pub gigs where the only payment is a free drink or a share of the money taken on the door. A large portion of profiles on these sites are dormant, suggesting that users often register and then rarely use them to find work in practice.

Disciplining musicians

In original music, the workforce was already tightly disciplined without digitalized intermediaries. While, for function gigs, musicians we interviewed in London had strong and consistent views on what constituted an acceptable price (usually £150 per band member), musicians looking to perform their own creative work almost never did. Indeed, the same individuals will often perform both kinds of work on different nights of the week. When asked, they can be quite explicit about expecting good pay for one type of job and almost nothing for the other. So, in original music, is there much need for the marketizing impetus of the platform model? Musicians' own desire to perform as an end in itself is often discipline enough (Umney and Kretsos, 2014).

In function work, it's a different story. Consider this guidance about how to approach clients posted by one of the digitalized agencies.

Apart from the gigging essentials such as refreshments and a place to get changed, etc., do you share our ethos that you are booked as a paid 'service' to the client and their guests (no different to caterers, florists or photographers)? **We have a ZERO DIVA policy** (we actually find the best musicians just get on with it). No other profession gets fed at work or demands hot meals on arrival. Of course, if you are at a venue for a long time (or have to set-up early) then of course we request a meal for you but it should always be seen as a bonus and never 'demanded' from our clients. (Music companies do talk to each other about band behaviour and some do have blacklists). *When chatting to brides and grooms at wedding fayres, we hear time and time again that the single biggest thing that puts them off the idea of live music is the pre-conceived idea that bands (particularly singers) are 'too demanding or too much hassle'.* (bold and italics in original) (Azzellini et al., 2021: 15)

The message here is that many musicians should reduce their expectations of clients in terms of food; and if they don't, they risk being blacklisted. Enterprises may perceive musicians' norms about proper treatment as a problem from the perspective of their business model. Digitalized agencies also sometimes violate established rules of thumb about pricing (not to mention union guideline rates, which are slightly higher). By facilitating quick price comparisons, these sites create a strong and clear incentive to lower fees, as a means of attracting buyers. Managers at digitalized intermediaries sometimes advise acts that reducing their price is the best strategy for getting more work, and digitalized agencies often have acts available for well beneath the £150 per member going rate (which we found to be a fairly widespread rule of thumb among musicians doing function work). One leading UK site, for instance, during our research period was featuring four-piece bands with a starting price of £100 for the entire group (so £25 per member, which is significantly less than national minimum wage if we consider that a wedding function might take several hours accounting for travel and waiting times). The rates on this site, however, were unusually low, and at many others the number of acts smashing through the £150 floor was lower, suggesting that many function musicians were not giving up on going rates just yet.

Digitalized agencies put additional downward pressure on musicians' prices by reducing their ability to negotiate. When signing up to a digitalized agency, they are required to post a price at which they will be advertised. They can adjust this as they choose, by editing their profile. But whatever is displayed is the price that buyers see. Although this is only a starting price, with add-ons subject to the contingencies of the gig, it does reduce musicians' flexibility to negotiate higher bespoke fees from gig to gig. Managers at digitalized agencies explicitly discourage musicians from negotiating higher fees and not only because they consider it insufficiently customer-friendly. It also slows down the transaction, requiring additional emails, when the business model is based on volume and speed of transactions. Consequently, function bands will work for similar prices irrespective of the buyer, whether it is a family party or a corporate event where champagne is circulating for thousands of pounds per bottle. A more traditional agent would not reveal musicians' prices like this. Instead, they would typically negotiate on a client-by-client basis. Hence another disciplinary effect of digitalized marketization is the disappearance of the musicians' prerogative to negotiate.

Digitalized agencies often also impose rules on musicians intended to bind them more tightly into a particular marketplace. For instance, they sometimes forbid acts from handing out their own business cards on gigs. In practice, it's not difficult for musicians to evade this instruction. But the aim is to preserve the agency's position as the organizer of market exchange. The musician, on the other hand, loses an opportunity to build personal contacts that could restore to them some control over the transaction. Agencies may also impose up-front costs and risk on musicians, such as when they require them to invest in their glossy promotional materials with no guarantee of a return on this outlay (which are often a pre-requisite for acts joining the roster).

Finally, also note that the market mechanisms created by digitalized agencies tend to escape established mechanisms of democratic accountability. We are not talking here about the bureaucracy built in marketized health and welfare systems to minimize public oversight; it would be melodramatic to accuse live music agencies of 'subverting democracy' in this way. However, the digitalized agencies discussed here are substantially less likely, for instance, to be part of the collective bargaining systems that may apply to traditional agents or respect the informal norms of live musicians themselves. There are no collectively agreed standards around commission rates, and managers at digitalized agencies openly acknowledge how easy it would be for them to charge even 100 per cent commissions. So digitalized agencies do in fact reduce *industrial democracy*, that is the scope for workers to have a collective say over how their industry is run.

Indeed, musicians are often unaware of what kind of profits agents are making, and this can vary widely between engagements without their knowledge. A digitalized agency, alongside the online selection system, might also have other avenues for booking bands, such as the following: a client submits an enquiry form specifying their requirements for a gig, as well as their budget. The agent may then ring round a series of acts directly, asking them what fee they will do the gig for, without telling them the client's budget. They will offer the lowest bidder to the client, who in the meantime knows how much they have offered to pay, but not what the band's fee is. The agent can thus rack up significant margins unbeknownst to both the band and the client. So while digitalized agencies generally make profits by creating more open and ostensibly transparent marketplaces, they can simultaneously pursue covert profit-making strategies that depend on participants lacking information and discussions taking place offline.

All of this tells us, on one hand, that digitalization has been an important means of intensifying price competition and thus instilling class discipline on the function music workforce. On the other hand, however, we can't say that the platform model has been a genuinely 'disruptive' force (to adopt the jargon of the platform economy). Few sites we examined had the functionality of a platform, and those that did were on the non-lucrative margins of the live music business. This sector also once again exemplifies the point that the intensity of competition is not simply determined by the number of buyers and sellers in a sector. It is conceivable that some platform or digitalized agency will come to dominate the sector and act as a monopolist. But that would not eliminate competition: it would rather mean that monopolist gets to act as the organizer of competition.

Limits to the platform economy

This takes us back to an observation made earlier in this chapter: a rapid and complete shift to a fully automated platform model is not an effective way of achieving class discipline in live music. More partial and hybrid forms of digitalization are more effective, in part because the enterprise maintains control over competition and can orchestrate it on its own terms.

In this case, the limits of the platform model are not because it imposes too much market, as in the Polanyian argument, but because of the nature of existing market relations. We showed how platforms struggled because the market was so fragmented and higher-value market segments still depend on personal contact networks. This is because the nature of the transaction was too complex and contingent to automate, and because the methods of providing instant comparability between musicians were unconvincing to market participants. It is these features of markets, rather than any social countermovement against marketization, which matters most.

A simpler explanation for the limits of platformization in live music is that firms are not seeking to innovate digitally for the sake of doing so. They are, instead, looking to accelerate market competition *on their terms*. This is a complicated and often labour-intensive process requiring the construction of new mechanisms and processes. Technological fixes can help with this in some ways, but less so in others. In live music, marketizers have had to struggle against the various factors we have mentioned, which are less dramatic but just as obstructive as the kinds of protest and non-compliance seen in health and welfare systems. Digitalization only goes so far in responding, and human oversight remains important in order to maintain control of the marketization process.

We can reiterate some of the organizational and technical barriers to platformization in live music. First, the transaction itself is extremely complicated. A function gig features an array of contingencies which demand interpersonal negotiation. When booking a wedding band, much needs to be thrashed out. Is the gig easy for the band to get to? How much will transportation cost? What equipment do the band have to bring? Will they need to wait around a long time after setting up? What happens if the performance is delayed (e.g. if speeches overrun)? Will food be provided or do bands have to make their own arrangements?

Do the band have to rehearse specific songs, for example, for a first dance? These questions are all sufficiently awkward and complex that an automated system has yet to be devised that can deal with them. As such, human oversight of transactions remains ineradicable.

Second, live music is so fragmented that it has, so far, been insurmountably difficult to create a genuine 'one-stop shop' that can be used across all of its domains. Function and original gigs are linked insofar as the same individuals may work in both. But apart from this, there are huge variations. The kinds of venues and audiences involved, the kinds of services being offered, the manner in which musicians need to advertise themselves and hence the kinds of promotional materials they will upload, the assumptions around pricing: these all vary. The failure to unify the market is not for want of trying. Gigmit, for instance, has previously sought to branch into function work, but without much success, partly because they just aren't trusted by the big players in the function world, such as hotel chains and events companies (Azzellini et al., 2021).

Third, judgements of value in live music are irreducibly qualitative. The use of data-driven ranking systems remains quite unconvincing in live music. Live music is often a thrill, whose vibrancy comes from intangible factors like atmosphere and energy, and this is near impossible to encapsulate numerically. On most digitalized agencies, star systems may exist but often appear half-hearted. Few acts received more than a handful of ratings, so mechanisms for ranking bands according to popularity are unreliable. To assess the quality of acts, customers have to comb through embedded video and audio files. This is surely a more nuanced way of gauging the quality of musicians than through star ratings systems, but it is also more cumbersome and time-consuming.

The job of marketizing live music work is progressing but incomplete. Its incompleteness isn't due to societal resistance to excessive market but the inherent difficulty of extending market competition in the first place. The 'progress' towards marketization which has been made so far has had clear and unambiguous disciplinary effects. Digital technologies have been means to this end but are unable to resolve all the complexities of staging price competition, and will even be discarded if they are not directly useful to agencies' extraction of profits. Of course, in early 2020, the situation for everyone involved in live music changed dramatically for the worse, and at the time of writing (early 2022) is only gradually recovering.

Covid-19 and marketization in live music

The effects of the Covid-19 lockdowns on live music were grimly overwhelming and for many music careers a near-extinction event. The pandemic and its social effects have forced musicians to leave the industry or else face the prospect of subsisting on a tiny fraction of their previous income[3]. At the time of writing, it is too early to say much about what the industry's revival will look like, but some observations need to be made about the immediate impact of Covid.

The work of consolidating a marketplace for function musicians was set back by the pandemic, since demand for live music halted overnight. Exchange in this market suddenly stopped completely. Presumably, this work is recommencing as restrictions ease. But in the meantime, it is important to note what has happened among the scattered fragments of the live music sector.

In lockdown, live musicians suddenly had to find alternative sources of income. For many, this simply meant doing more work outside of live music, such as teaching lessons over Zoom. But there were also improvised technological fixes to enable people to keep performing and potentially monetize it. Subscription services like Patreon became important for some. Musicians can give certain subscribers access to exclusive performances and recordings, along with other forms

---

[3] See 'Coronavirus presses mute button on music industry' News item on Musicians' Union website available at https://musiciansunion.org.uk/Home/News/2020/Sep/Coronavirus-Presses-Mute-Button-on-Music-Industry (accessed 12 September 2020).

of privileged material (such as videos and texts outlining the artist's practice regime or documenting rehearsals).

For those without a fanbase devoted enough to make Patreon-style models lucrative, another method is live-streaming performances over widely used platforms such as Facebook or YouTube. For many, this is essentially a form of online busking. A tip jar app is sometimes used to give live-stream viewers the option of donating a discretionary amount. This exposed and compounded the vast hierarchies within live music, because established names were able to raise relatively large sums of money in this way, with others scrabbling for change.

What kind of market dynamics pertain in these kinds of cases? Certainly, lockdown meant fierce competition for eyeballs and clicks. But this competition was not yet being orchestrated in the same way as digitalized agencies orchestrate competition for function work. This activity is far more DIY. Most musicians did not find it lucrative, but still, by disseminating live-streamed performances through their networks of friends and supporters they were often able to get some kind of income and perhaps also managed to maintain people's awareness of their continued existence during months of isolation. They also used live-streamed events to instigate new collaborations to broaden these support networks further, for instance, by having multi-person performances, either socially distanced in a large room or by assembling remote contributions from performers in different locations. So there was solidarity and mutual aid at work in coping with the pandemic.

But musicians we interviewed expressed significant worries, as well. For many professional musicians, the 'pay as you feel' model was subject to many reservations, particularly on the grounds that it threatens to normalize playing for free. Admittedly, this was already widespread in many areas of live music, but numerous professional musicians were still holding out. One musician contact we caught up with during lockdown made the following observation: many artists who had previously criticized the pay-as-you-feel model had, literally overnight and more or less without protest, come to accept it. What else can you do, in a pandemic? The question, though, is whether this forced lowering of musicians' expectations is going to have a lasting effect, even as the industry eventually revives. If so, then the pandemic will prove to have been a more powerful instrument of class discipline in live music than online platforms ever could.

7

Beyond marketization

In the first half of this book, we spelled out a critical theory of marketization. We argued not only against the idea held by some economists that market exchange is part of the human condition but also against theories that dismissively treat marketization as unlikely or unimportant. In this chapter, we focus on the limits of marketization, because we think they point to the vulnerabilities of contemporary capitalism. Is marketization curtailed by pragmatic politicians who recognize that market competition is not always the best way to organize transactions? Are some countries or contexts relatively immune to marketization? Is it always likely to produce some kind of social backlash that 're-embeds' it?

Our response is no. Many of the measures we recounted in Chapters 4 and 5 could not reasonably be described as 'pragmatic'. Marketization has been a complex and laborious process that has persisted despite many problems and in circumstances where it might have been more pragmatic to reverse course. Market mechanisms have been imposed forcefully in countries that are supposed to be less market-oriented. While in some cases – particularly in healthcare – social movements have challenged and limited marketization, we are more pessimistic about this as a general trend than Polanyians. Indeed, we have shown how, often, market-making is conducted in quiet and technocratic ways to defuse opposition. We also criticized what we called the 'Goldilocks' view, where state and market are seen as opposite ends of a sliding scale. We have seen that marketization can be a highly 'statist' process, not only in which central governments attempt to dismantle established (non-market) arrangements but also in which they create new competition-enhancing arrangements. This takes place in a variety of countries, including those thought to have non-liberal forms of capitalism, like France and Germany.

Marketization is the process of intensifying price-based competition, particularly by eliminating barriers to market entry, increasing comparability between market participants and increasing the frequency of transactions. This is not simply opposed to monopoly or monopsony.[1] In a monopoly, competition is limited on one plane, but the monopolist may orchestrate competition more intensively on another. So marketization is inseparable from questions of power in exchange. It's a story of capitalists and the state managing the exchange process and the opportunities for profit-making and securing a return on investment that most markets require. Governments sometimes commit to protecting workers and citizens to protect them in the face of intense market competition, but these protections are also being swept aside deliberately by states as part of the general liberalization trend described by Baccaro and Howell (2017).

It would be misguided to describe marketization as a cunning capitalist plot. Often it achieves underwhelming and frustrating results for all concerned. In health and welfare we recounted various examples of deadlocks, stalemates and dead ends that frustrated profit-making. We argued in Chapter 3 that, to explain its odd persistence in twenty-first-century Europe, we need to recognize the way changes in international political economy, including the enhanced urgency of ensuring 'business confidence', have pressured states to think of class discipline as an end in itself. This helps to explain the commitment to marketization policies despite disappointing outcomes: it may sometimes be a cynical scheme to realize profits at the expense of the rest of society, but more often it is a sincere if damaging response to unstable political-economic conditions by politicians who genuinely believe in the benign powers of 'the market'.

---

[1] The point about the compatibility between monopsony and competition is also well made by Kumar (2020).

By contrast, in live music, private enterprises went about reorganizing exchange themselves. In some cases they were pragmatic, using digital technologies to extend their business model, but without automating transactions or creating a multi-sided marketplace. This allowed digitalized agencies to maintain their role in coordinating and controlling exchange in the face of complex contingencies (especially for function musicians), while taking advantage of the broader reach of online tools. But in other cases, we did find attempts to impose a platform model on live music markets. These were confined to the bottom end of the market, with few transactions and low prices, stifled by the inherently qualitative valuation of live music (especially for the performance of original music) and the fragmented nature of the organizational field. In these situations where we expected online platforms to be a vector of marketization, market conditions were shaping the progress of technological change, rather than the other way round.

Even where they did not live up to the expectations of their creators, these markets intensified competition in a way that disciplined workers. Digitalized entertainment agencies and front-line advisors in work-first employment services encouraged workers to lower their expectations about working conditions. DRGs and competitive tendering imposed new imperatives and criteria on health and welfare workers that often devalued or sped up what they did. Through algorithms or through bureaucracy, these marketization cases insulated the market from democratic accountability and political oversight.

Our book and our theory have focused on inequality but in a particular form. It has examined the power disparity between workers and capital. We have not explicitly discussed other kinds of inequality, such as disparities by gender, disability or race. Nonetheless, it is clear that the class disciplinary effects we identify are likely, in many cases, to be disproportionately damaging to people already experiencing intersecting forms of oppression (Lee and Tapia, 2021). The most blatant example of this is punitive active labour-market policies. In the United Kingdom, policymakers targeted disabled people and lone parents. In the United States, where workfare policies were pioneered, the motivation was to win over white voters to Republican candidates (Kohler-Hausmann, 2017), and it has disproportionately targeted Black women (Soss et al., 2011).

But workfare is not the only example in our data. Consider the healthcare workforce, for instance: the professions that were most fiercely disciplined by marketization in our account were front-line roles such as nursing, which are more likely to be done by women. By contrast, services such as specialized surgery, which were likely to be lucrative under marketization, are more likely to be carried out by men. There are many ways in which the inequality entrenched by class discipline is likely to intersect with and exacerbate other inequalities, and we have not been able to fully do them justice here.

In this final chapter, we consider the wider political scene, reflecting on what alternatives may be to marketization and what are the prospects that they might be realized.

The centre–left and the market

Polanyi argued that the creation of markets involves more central planning than social protection. This is as much the case in our lifetimes as it was in his. Resistance to marketization – and alternatives to it – are unplanned and normally invisible to or disdained by elite opinion formers.

It is common for American-centric accounts of the neoliberal turn to associate it with the 'radical right' and think tanks bankrolled by the wealthy supplying policy prescriptions to increasingly disciplined Republican lawmakers (MacLean, 2017). In Europe, the situation is different, in part because of the obvious role that ostensibly 'nonpartisan' European elites have played in the events above. Consider the 'Troika', a consortium of institutions that sought to make an example of the leftist Greek government after the financial crisis. They were appointed technocrats deliberately sealed off from politics, not politicians swept into power on a right-wing populist wave funded by billionaires.

Another reason for this difference, though, is the role of the centre–left in liberalization policies in Europe. The Hartz reforms in Germany, the abolition of Incapacity Benefits and rise of a for-profit employment services industry in Britain, and the decades-long march towards profit-making in England's National Health Service were all important marketization initiatives mentioned earlier supported or initiated by centre–left governments. The intellectual justification for these policies was based around a particular version of the Goldilocks theory that we identified in the introduction. Left parties had previously been too close to the state end of the spectrum, and what was needed was a new balance a little bit more towards the market. This was supported with much rhetoric about how a new wave of social-democratic parties had turned into sceptics of 'big government' and advocates of private-sector expansion, keen to end the 'bureaucracy' of 'top–down' public services.

The irony is that marketization initiatives have in many cases required a more overbearing state and trampled on smaller-scale local alternatives. An excellent example comes from the British employment services market, where top–down marketization initiatives drove innovative community-based non-profit organizations out of the field and replaced them with larger commercial organizations that were more responsive to the incentive structure. While justified as ways to seek better 'value for money', they have frequently proven inefficient and costly. Julian Le Grand proposed quasi-markets as a way that governments could break the entrenched power of public-sector workers and put their customers first. The unfortunate reality of marketized public services is bureaucratic bloat, pressures to put investors first, and problems with service quality, including the systematic neglect of the neediest service users.

Centre–left governments have branded themselves not as opponents of marketization, but as competent implementers, concerned with equality and transparency. They have attempted to make the process more equitable by providing some kind of compensation or safety net for the 'losers' of marketization. Workers may be made unemployed by privatization or free trade, but at least there are government programmes to help them find work; these programmes may force them into low-wage jobs, but at least there is a national minimum wage; their right to strike may be sharply curtailed, but at least the government encourages labour-management cooperation to improve competitiveness. As regards efficiency, centre–left parties often accuse right-wing counterparts of incompetence and corruption in their management of marketization initiatives. The UK Labour Party, for instance, has made cronyism a major thrust of its critique of the Conservative government's governance of NHS outsourcing, particularly during the pandemic (Geoghegan, 2020). Implicitly, the important question is how to manage public services in line with market-centred rules, not whether to do so. Is this really the line of critique people on the left want to take? One which leaves largely unquestioned the moral and intellectual case for marketization?

We hope that, with this book, we have shown why wishing for a more equitable and transparent version of marketization is misguided. Marketization cannot be transparent because of the complex choices involved and the practical difficulties that follow when these choices are politicized. Lack of democratic accountability is a feature, not a bug, of marketization. Market mechanisms, even those executed competently and without nepotism, are still opaque and sheltered from oversight from workers and the wider public.

Are there other ideas within centre–left policy circles that help point beyond marketization? The most influential voices, such as Joseph Stiglitz or Thomas Piketty, are focused on questions of redistribution via taxation. Income inequality is identified as the main problem, and the response should be to recognize it as such and adjust tax rates accordingly. Piketty has been highly vocal and ambitious in plans for a wealth tax (Piketty, 2014), and Stiglitz has bemoaned the spiteful and counterproductive way that elites handled the Greek debt crisis (Stiglitz, 2016). This discussion of inequality and taxation, however, remains within the logic of 'compensating the losers' and neglects qualitative problems of power, dignity and voice. While many on the centre–left have supported fights against other forms of inequality, such as Me Too or Black Lives Matter, they have been slower to reject market dogmas which entrench gendered and racial disparities, and which force people into low-paid jobs and devalue work based on care, to give but two examples.

Other economists, such as Mariana Mazzucato, propose solutions that go well beyond the tax system. Mazzucato's work has become increasingly important and influenced some politicians on the left, popularizing the notion of the 'entrepreneurial state'. This included the UK Labour Party under Jeremy Corbyn's leadership, which for a time was one of a small number of mainstream European left parties curious about alternatives to marketization.

LaPlane and Mazzucato (2020) explicitly reject the idea of the state as 'market corrector', that is as something that is there to intervene only when a market goes demonstrably wrong. The state should not just fix markets but 'actively co-create them'. They thus see state and market as symbiotic, rather than opposing poles. Much of the neoliberal policy consensus in favour of markets, they suggest, reflects an intellectual error, a failure to perceive the necessary and desirable symbiosis between market and state. Like us, they criticize the notion of a polarity between market and state. In their view, however, this symbiosis can be progressive, where the state actively involves itself in high-risk investments throughout cutting-edge value chains and recoups a larger share of the rewards accordingly. Governments investing in green technology, for example, could claim a bigger share of the eventual profits and do more to ensure that resulting innovations are widely available.

What are the implications of this argument for analyses of marketization? LaPlane and Mazzucato criticize an over-reliance on market mechanisms without enough public involvement or benefit. Key elements of marketizing policy agendas – such as encouraging private provision – would appear to be thwarted by the invigorated public sector they advocate. But a more strategic, empowered and 'entrepreneurial' state could just as easily be one that wields the discipline of price competition ferociously within its own supply chains, as it seeks urgent technological fixes to problems from pandemics to climate change. Deliberately making and governing markets is similar to Le Grand's proposals from the 1990s and what governments have done when marketizing employment services and health services, and the aim was often to tighten government control over those services.

For us, of course, marketization is not only a bad idea: it is bound up with the material force of class discipline. Converting elites to the gospel of Polanyi will not make much of a difference. Even if a left government came to power next week promising a total reversal of marketization, it would not do so in practice. The imperative to discipline workers is not an ideological blunder but a real consequence of neoliberalism and financialization. This was the argument we made in Chapter 3. This prerogative of capitalist states, however, does not mean that marketization is an unassailable force wielded by an unshakeable nexus of state and capital. We have argued throughout this book that it is a much more dysfunctional process than this, characterized by frequent wasted effort, dead ends and unexpected resistance. The next section discusses the practical implications of this point, which are not in grand designs to reform government financing or economic development policy, but rather in the everyday lives of ordinary people.

The dysfunctions of marketization and their uses

Repeatedly, both marketizing public administrators and private businesses hoping to profit from marketization told us they were frustrated by politics. These politics could be noisy and visible, as when workers and patients protest the privatization of a hospital, or quiet and obscure, as when a committee of local policymakers meets to decide whether to continue an experiment with for-profit employment services. Opposition to marketization did not take the form of some central plan to nationalize the economy and reduce the discipline of the labour market on workers. Nevertheless, marketization requires depoliticization (or at least 'quiet politics'), and where this is impossible, marketization is rendered brittle. Opponents of marketization need to make quiet politics noisy.

One example of highly visible forms of politicization are the protests against local commissioning groups in the English NHS, which the government intended to be the institutional cutting edge of marketization. The plans to open the market to private providers have only proceeded incrementally, and in numerous cases have been beaten back. As Genevieve Coderre-Lapalme's research has shown, this is because these commissioning institutions met visible and audible local political opposition from trade unions and public campaigners, and local politicians (Coderre-LaPalme, 2018). This kind of local political contestation repeatedly led to the collapse of privatization initiatives.

But politics also interfered in other, less obvious ways. Front-line workers in health and welfare services often maintained professional identities and priorities which conflicted with the new incentive priorities set down by marketization. This is a question of *workplace politics*: a quieter but no less critical relative of the politics of public protest. The fact that a hospital reform, for instance, formally incentivizes 'productivity' metrics such as shorter stays does not mean that staff only think about discharging patients as quickly as possible. Staff have their own ideas about how their job should be done, and the political questions that arise when this is threatened are vital for the effective (or not) implementation of marketization. Resistance to marketization is an enduring part of everyday working life (Sanson and Courpasson, 2022).

Workplace politics were most obvious in cases of health and welfare, but were also relevant to our study of live musicians, even though the marketizers here were private businesses, not the state. Recall how intensified competition threatened going rates for function gigs. But these going rates were not simply eradicated. While some sites advertised numerous bands with lower prices, price norms still held fairly well up on many others. Musicians' own ideas about proper professional treatment don't just disappear. In the context of marketization, they become vital political questions at work. This is made clearly apparent by looking at the emergence of Facebook groups with names like 'Stop Working for Free' and 'Gig Food – the Highs and the Lows', which provide an online space in which these politics can be incubated and sustained in the workplace and in the marketplace.

These politics also mattered for the digitalized agencies, which were staffed by musicians and people with close ties to the music industry. These connections tended to constrain profit extraction: while some agencies told us that they *could* extract 100 per cent commissions, for instance, very few of them admitted they *would*. (Only one of our interviewees at live music agencies explicitly told us about doing so; the rest said forcefully that they wouldn't). The everyday implications of that policy for the market would have become a problem for them and would have troubled their sense of ethics. The sensitivities of workplace politics either limit profit extraction or at least force it into covert channels. As a general rule, more people understanding more about what is going on makes marketization more difficult.

Just as the politics of protest and the politics of work and exchange run interference on marketization, so too do administrative politics. Our research also showed how administrators in public services sometimes declined to comply with the spirit of new marketizing reforms or at least complied with them in an unenthusiastic manner. This was often not a question of ideology but of pragmatism: ignoring market strictures may lead to better and cheaper services, especially where the central state does not effectively impose the market. In French welfare-to-work systems, for instance, the managers at small non-profit providers built organizational networks with other non-profits because they had evolved their services through collaboration. They knew how the other, quite specialized organizations around them operated and knew how their own services fit in. So they would tend to direct service users around this network. This practice continued despite central attempts to integrate for-profit multinationals into the system. Advocates of the latter sometimes construed this as ideological prejudice (a common argument runs: 'French providers and policymakers are nepotistic, set in their ways, and aren't innovative or open to new ideas'), but for people within the incumbent organizations it was equally a pragmatic choice to work with established and proven collaborators when handling difficult situations. This was combined with a lack of trust towards large for-profit providers which was not rooted in superstition, but based on evaluation evidence and experience.

We previously said that marketization should not be considered unassailable. Now, we need the opposite warning. Our discussion of the politics of marketization is not meant to make it seem toothless. It just shows how politics can interfere with marketization at multiple levels. This does not mean that marketization will automatically be rolled back or even necessarily face resistance; indeed, marketizers tend to deliberately seal the process off from political interference, if the policymaking process itself is not already too complex and opaque to achieve attention, protest and 'salience'. As industrial relations authors commonly argue, the decline of unions is a serious barrier to mounting resistance to the neoliberal drift of institutions and countering it requires re-building collective working-class power (Doellgast et al., 2018). Despite union decline and the lack of robust alternatives from centre–left parties and their intellectual supporters, politicization is a problem for marketizers. Although much effort goes into insulating marketization efforts from politics, marketizers and privatizers have varying levels of success. So one objective for opponents of marketization has been to render its 'quiet politics' audible.

Marketization is also dysfunctional for other reasons. Its organizational mechanics are often awkward, and the promise of profits is sometimes disappointing. Note that this is not necessarily because of the economic axiom that competition squeezes profits. In healthcare, for instance, it reflects how impoverished the 'marketplace' became under austerity, and in the most austere health marketplace we examined, that of Greece, gaps in provision were being met by solidarity clinics that operated on a radically non-commercial basis. (When we asked one public hospital administrator whether he was competing for patients, he told us that because of shortages of staff and supplies the hospital would benefit from having fewer, and not more, patients.) To create a crowded and competitive market, the transactions on offer need to attract participants, and expectations of future profits are centrally important for this. Austerity is an oft-cited pretext and cause of marketization, since the retreat of the state is thought to lead to the extension of the market. But we found that austerity could also stunt marketization.

To put it bluntly, some elements of marketization contradict other elements, making it a brittle process in many cases. Another example of this is the tension between competition-stimulating funding systems and decentralization, as two mutually contradictory forms of marketization in French healthcare (see Chapter 3). Again, this is not to advise complacency about marketization. Quite the opposite: its dysfunctionality does not prevent the damage it does.

Followers of Michel Foucault make an important point when they emphasize that in a 'neoliberal' society, market competition plays a central role in structuring everyday life. Whether people are successful in the market or whether markets function as advertised matters less for them than the point that subjectivity changes. Our interviewees in French hospitals spoke of 'privatization of the spirit' to describe how their working patterns were changing to respond to DRG incentives. However, this language would seem to downplay the problem. A job seeker forced to choose between accepting a low-wage job and losing unemployment benefits; a nurse who will not receive a pay increase because her workplace has been outsourced or privatized; and a musician advised by his digitalized agent to advertise a lower fee: all of these individuals would be lucky to experience marketization only in spirit. Marketization cannot be understood separately from the power relations between classes that determine it and the distribution of wealth and income that result from it. And its dysfunctions allow us to glimpse a world beyond it.

Non-market orders, planned and unplanned

We cannot give a blueprint for a left government to reverse the damage of the past decades. Not only because this would involve generalizations too simple to have practical relevance and visionary proposals that would never be implemented, but also because in reality non-market forms of organization normally emerge without a blueprint. This is a key Polanyian insight, but unlike Polanyians we centralize questions of class power and class discipline in understanding marketization and its outcomes. The strategy we propose is one of creating spaces for spontaneous non-market orders to emerge and develop, and supporting and amplifying some of them when they do. It will be difficult to predict whether the result is a credible and desirable alternative to marketization, although in our view freedom from market discipline is in itself desirable. It is therefore important to scrutinize real-world alternatives.

In our study of health and welfare services, we have shown how marketization has been repeatedly driven through by the central state, and has either overridden or been hindered by, initiatives by local groups and organizations. Does this, therefore, mean an embrace of localism and a 'small is beautiful' philosophy that identifies marketization with the central state?

In some cases it might, but we do not advance small-scale localism as the solution. Localism informs important recent policy ideas on the left, such as the 'anchor institution' model (often referred to as the 'Cleveland model' in the United States and the 'Preston model' in the United Kingdom and promoted by think tanks such as the Democracy Collaborative). This involves designating key local institutions, with a big weight in the local economy (such as universities or major hospitals) as 'anchor institutions' (Alperovitz et al., 2010). These organizations have a huge impact locally because they constantly purchase services such as cleaning, laundry, catering and driving. To be an anchor institution means that these institutions cannot threaten to exit a local community, and their resulting dependence on it creates an incentive for them to use their financial might to improve their local area. Instead of purchasing goods and services from multinational corporations, for example, they could commit to working with small local firms or cooperatives to divert resources into their local economy. Indeed, a focus on cooperatives – which can fulfil various socially important functions such as employing ex-prisoners – is critical to much literature on the subject.

The 'Anchor Institutions' model seeks to bolster and formalize the role of local institutions and networks as a counterweight to the power of global capital. In this sense, it is an example of an unplanned non-marketized local order. In Cleveland, which is the most influential exemplar of anchor institutions in the United States, the emphasis has been to 'hire local, buy local, live local'. This means the largest employers tended, and encouraged their suppliers, to emphasize recruiting local residents, especially those from under-represented communities. They also directed purchasing dollars towards local firms, with an emphasis on cooperatives, with the aim of locking resources into the local community.

However, blunting marketization is not enough: it is necessary to reverse it. That means restoring and bolstering labour's class power. An anchor institution model could potentially serve this end. But in the case of Cleveland, power remained in the hands of the top management in the largest employers in the area; workers at the cooperatives continued to earn very low wages; and unions or workers centres lacked a prominent role. Promotion of collective bargaining, normalizing trade union membership and bolstering working-class power do not feature prominently in the Cleveland model. Indeed, part of its appeal to hospital and university administrators is institutional self-interest: its utility to improve the reputations of institutions that already have economic dominance in their cities.

It is therefore not surprising that leaders in these projects note that trade unions have been sceptical of these types of initiatives. A 'small is beautiful' ethos is often anathema to unions because small businesses can be profoundly opposed to collective bargaining and resistant to labour regulations. A diffuse tapestry of small firms could be substantially more challenging to unions and collective bargaining than a handful of large firms and public-sector entities, even if those small firms are socially minded local cooperatives. In the UK, partly because of its association with left-Labour councillors, labour issues appear to be more integrated into the anchor institution model, with stipulations around the Real Living Wage included in arrangements (McInroy, 2018). But they are likely to find themselves isolated both within their own party which has little interest in challenging marketization, not to mention within the wider British political landscape which is set to be dominated by further waves of austerity and marketization post Covid-19. There is also the thorny question of whether these models (and the emphasis on small local provision) would be co-opted as a form of 'nice' privatization, acceptable to the centre–left, which experience tells us would quickly fall for such a ruse. If the history of British employment services is any guide, this would be a bait-and-switch, in which a language of partnership with the voluntary and community sector is used to legitimize what turns out to be a transfer of services to multinational corporations (Davies, 2008).

Our research also revealed various kinds of solidaristic activity which kindled new forms of non-market relationships in a spontaneous way. The most obvious to us, given our personal histories, is the trade union movement, worker self-organization, works councils and worker control in production. Empowering professions in the public sector would have a similar effect (Lethbridge, 2019). It also includes the solidarity clinics we saw in Greece and the mutual support networks developing among musicians in the wake of Covid-19. These are unplanned forms of non-market activity which arise to resist or compensate for the failures of a capitalist society subordinated to the market. It is true that unions and large non-profits plan their own activities and sometimes act strategically, deploying their resources based on a well worked-out plan, backed up by research. However, there is no movement of working-class people coordinated at the scale of EU-wide markets. Working-class movements are often adept at resisting injustice and coping with failure, but they are not building an alternative political economy. Solidarity is spontaneous, markets are planned.

We do not accept the Foucauldian argument that neoliberalism necessarily implies a shift in rationality towards an embrace of the market. It does for some people, but we frequently met people rejecting this rationality, whether out of principles of solidarity or simply out of a desire to do what, in their view, is most effective. Moreover, at times, a non-market order grows, endures and thwarts marketization, at least temporarily. We saw this particularly in our study of welfare-to-work services in Seine-Saint-Denis, in the Parisian suburbs. Here, the roots of the network were sufficiently deep and sturdy that they had outlasted attempts to marketize the system. But in a neoliberal era, non-market arrangements are always potentially under threat, something of which our research participants were acutely aware.

Realistically, socialists are not currently in a position to set down a programme for government, at least not in the countries where we have lived and worked. However, what they can do is support, defend and create non-market activity. That means pooling and directing resources to support resistance by workers facing marketization and calling into question the rules of the market in those struggles. The quiet politics of market rule-making need to be made noisy, and hence easier to challenge. Consider how trade unions representing hospitals have started to explicitly problematize 'the meaning of work': in other words, they have campaigned in ways which directly juxtapose professional ethos with market logic and sought to show how market-centric rule changes threaten this. By doing this they can mobilize people. As Marx and Engels observed in *The Poverty of Philosophy*, worker struggles are not simply about trying to win a better wage; they are really about defending workers' humanity. The same is true of struggles against marketization.

This is a minimalist programme of action, but we can also comment on more ambitious top–down plans discussed by the contemporary left. Consider the current state of social policy debate, which on the left is focused either on defending existing welfare and social security systems or introducing a Universal Basic Income (UBI) (Calnitsky, 2017). While the former may provide life's necessities to vulnerable people, the latter gives them the spending power to freely choose what those necessities might be and purchase them on the market. UBI is an attractive option, since it could reduce pressure on workers to take low-quality jobs, provide an escape from the means tests and work requirements of the welfare state as we now know it, and enjoy support from across society as a universal benefit. In doing so, it would undermine a key vector of marketization and class discipline.

However, in other respects, UBI is compatible with, even supportive of, marketization. Certainly, where public services are inadequate, it would help working people purchase healthcare and education on the private market. Future governments could offer their populations UBI as a 'trade off' for privatization: 'You will have to buy your own healthcare from for-profit companies, but everyone will have money and can choose how to spend it!' If UBI were generous enough, it could loosen the discipline of the labour market on workers. On the other hand, it could also lurbricate exchange in markets for goods and services, and if it were set at a low enough level it could act as a subsidy for employers of low-wage workers, reinforcing class discipline.

Alternatively, consider a radicalized version of defending the existing welfare state: American proposals for job guarantees (Pressley and Stein, 2021), in which everyone who wants to work can find a living-wage job producing life's necessities, with the products available to all. This implies a more fundamental rolling back of marketization than UBI, because it involves democratic planning over what kind of work is done, leaving little room for opaque and insulated market rules in deciding how goods and services circulate. Moreover, by guaranteeing living-wage jobs and providing life's necessities, it greatly limits the scope of price competition as an organizing principle in society. The jobs guarantee is radically non-market, but it remains to be seen how it defines socially necessary work and how it avoids turning the right to work into a work requirement (see Lafargue, 1883).

It is now a convention in academic writing to treat the Covid-19 pandemic as a crisis that has exposed a problem that was not adequately recognized before, normally the problem that the writer would like to discuss. In the case of marketization, this exposure is unlikely to happen, because so much of it is submerged in the minutiae of government and corporate bureaucracy. For students of political economy, it is an interesting question how long (to paraphrase Keynes) the ideas of defunct neoliberal economists will continue to enslave the practical men and women who collectively decide what governments and corporations do. Meanwhile, punishing the poor, siphoning resources out of health systems and exploiting workers using apps and algorithms have compounded Covid-era suffering, all at a time when the struggle for survival of working-class people is at its most difficult.

References

Adams-Prassl, A., Boneva, T., Golin, M., & Rauh, C. (2020). Inequality in the impact of the coronavirus shock: Evidence from real time surveys. *CEPR Working Paper*.

Aglietta, M. (2000). Shareholder value and corporate governance: Some tricky questions. *Economy and Society, 29*(1), 146–159.

Alperovitz, G., Williamson, T., & Howard, T. (2010). The Cleveland model. *The Nation, 1*(1), 21–24.

Appelbaum, E., & Batt, R. (2014). *Private equity at work: When wall street manages main street*. Russell Sage Foundation.

Auffenberg, J. (2021). *Trade union strategies against healthcare marketization*. Routledge.

Azzellini, D., Greer, I., & Umney, C. (2021). Why isn't there an Uber for live music? The digitalisation of intermediaries and the limits of the platform economy. *New Technology, Work and Employment, 37*(1), 1–23.

Baccaro, L., & Howell, C. (2011). A common neoliberal trajectory: The transformation of industrial relations in advanced capitalism. *Politics & Society, 39*(4), 521–563.

Baccaro, L., & Howell, C. (2017). *Trajectories of neoliberal transformation: European industrial relations since the 1970s*. Cambridge University Press.

Baran, P. A., & Sweezy, P. M. (1968). *Monopoly capital: An essay on the American economic and social order*. Penguin Books.

Barbier, J-C., & Knuth, M. (2011). Activating social protection against unemployment: France and Germany compared. *Sozialer Fortschritt, 60*(1/2), 15–24.

Barrow, C. W. (1993). *Critical theories of the state: Marxist, Neomarxist, Postmarxist*. University of Wisconsin Press.

Barta, Z., & Johnston, A. (2018). Rating politics? Partisan discrimination in credit ratings in developed economies. *Comparative Political Studies, 51*(5), 587–620.

Benassi, C., & Dorigatti, L. (2015). Straight to the core – explaining union responses to the casualization of work: The IG Metall campaign for agency workers. *British Journal of Industrial Relations, 53*(3), 533–555.

Bender, G., & Kjellberg, A. (2021). A minimum-wage directive could undermine the Nordic model. *Social Europe*. https://socialeurope.eu/a -minimum-wage-directive-could-undermine-the-nordic-model

Bernaciak, M. (Ed.). (2015). *Market expansion and social dumping in Europe*. Routledge.

Berthet, T., & Bourgeois, C. (2016). The national governance of integrated activation policies in Europe. In Martin Heidenreich and Deborah Rice (Eds.), *Integrating social and employment policies in Europe* (211–234). Edward Elgar Publishing.

Bezes, P., & Le Lidec, P. (2011). L'hybridation du modèle territorial français. *Revue française d'administration publique, 136*(4), 919–942.

Bonefeld, W. (2004). On Postone's courageous but unsuccessful attempt to banish the class antagonism from the critique of political economy. *Historical Materialism, 12*(3), 103–124.

Bosch, G., & Weinkopf, C. (Eds.). (2008). *Low-wage work in Germany*. Russell Sage Foundation.

Bremmer, I. (2011). *End of the free market*. Portfolio.

Brenner, R. (2020). Escalating plunder. *New Left Review, 123*, 5–22.

Brinkmann, U., Dörre, K., & Röbenack, S. (2006). *Prekäre Arbeit. Ursachen, Ausmaß, soziale Folgen und subjektive Verarbeitungsformen unsicherer Beschäftigungsverhältnisse*. Friedrich Ebert Stiftung.

Burger, L. & Gould, J. (2013). Rhoen-Klinikum to sell hospitals to Fresenius for $4 billion. *Reuters*.

Butler, P. (2022). Universal credit claimants face tough sanctions in UK job crackdown. *The Guardian*, 27 January 2022.

Calnitsky, D. (2017). Debating basic income. *Catalyst, 1*(3), 63–90.

Campbell, J. & Pedersen, O. (2014). *The national origins of policy ideas: Knowledge regimes in the United States, France, Germany, and Denmark*. Princeton University Press.

Card, D., Kluve, J., & Weber, A. (2018). What works? A meta analysis of recent active labor market program evaluations. *Journal of the European Economic Association, 16*(3), 894–931.

Card, D., & Krueger, A. B. (2015). *Myth and measurement: The new economics of the minimum wage*. Princeton University Press.

Castel, R. (2017). *From manual workers to wage laborers: Transformation of the social question*. Routledge.

Chandra, P., & Chandra, P. (2020). Health care, technology, and socialized medicine. *Socialist Register, 57*, 257–273.

Coderre-Lapalme, G. (2018). Local trade union responses in the context of public healthcare service privatization. Doctoral dissertation, University of Greenwich.

Coderre-Lapalme, G., Greer, I., & Auffenberg, J. (2020). Fighting privatization in German and English health services: Union strategy, market structure, and campaign success. Manuscript.

Coderre-LaPalme, G., Greer, I., & Schulte, L. (2021). Welfare, work and the conditions of social solidarity: British campaigns to defend healthcare and social security. *Work, Employment and Society*.

Commons, J. R. (1906). Types of American labor unions--the musicians of St. Louis and New York. *The Quarterly Journal of Economics, 20*(3), 419–442.

Cook, D. (2018). *Adorno, Foucault and the critique of the west*. Verso Trade.

Crichton, T. (2021). Matt Hancock affair 'tip of the iceberg' in Tory crony contacts scandal, claims Scottish Labour MP. *Daily Record*.

Culpepper, P. D. (2010). *Quiet politics and business power: Corporate control in Europe and Japan*. Cambridge University Press.

Daguerre, A. (2014). New corporate elites and the erosion of the Keynesian social compact. *Work, Employment and Society, 28*(2), 323–334.

Dardot, P., & Laval, C. (2010). Néolibéralisme et subjectivation capitaliste. *Cités, 1*, 35–50.

Dardot, P., & Laval, C. (2014). *The new way of the world: On neoliberal society*. Verso.

Davies, S. (2008). Contracting out employment services to the third and private sectors: A critique. *Critical Social Policy, 28*(2), 136–164.

De Brunhoff, S. (2016). *Marx on money*. Verso Books.

Department for Work and Pensions (2015). Mortality statistics: Employment and support allowance, incapacity benefit or severe disablement allowance.

Doellgast, V. (2012). *Disintegrating democracy at work*. Cornell University Press.

Doellgast, V., & Greer, I. (2007). Vertical disintegration and the disorganization of German industrial relations 1. *British Journal of Industrial Relations, 45*(1), 55–76.

Doellgast, V., Lillie, N., & Pulignano, V. (Eds.). (2018). *Reconstructing solidarity: Labour unions, precarious work, and the politics of institutional change in Europe*. Oxford University Press.

Dörre, K., Scherschel, K., Booth, M., Haubner, T., Marquardsen, K., & Schierhorn, K. (2013). *Bewährungsproben für die Unterschicht?: Soziale Folgen aktivierender Arbeitsmarktpolitik*. Campus Verlag.

Dupuis, M., & Greer, I. (2021). Recentralizing industrial relations? local unions and the politics of insourcing in three North American automakers. *ILR Review*.

Ferber, T. (2015). *Bewertungskriterien und-matrizen im Vergabeverfahren: Wie erziele ich ein optimales Zuschlagsergebnis?*. Bundesanzeiger Verlag GmbH.

Finn, D. (2000). Welfare to work: The local dimension. *Journal of European Social Policy, 10*(1), 43–57.

Fleming, P., Rhodes, C., & Yu, K. H. (2019). On why Uber has not taken over the world. *Economy and Society, 48*(4), 488–509.

Fretel, A. (2013). La notion d'accompagnement dans les dispositifs de la politique d'emploi: entre centralité et indétermination. *Revue française de socio-économie, 1*, 55–79.

Freud, D. (2007). *Reducing dependency, increasing opportunity: Options for the future of welfare to work*. DWP.

Friedli, L., & Stearn, R. (2015). Positive affect as coercive strategy: Conditionality, activation and the role of psychology in UK government workfare programmes. *Medical Humanities, 41*(1), 40–47.

Friedman, M. (2001). How to cure health care. *Public Interest, 142*, 3.

Galbraith, J. K. (2008). *The predator state: How conservatives abandoned the free market and why liberals should too*. Simon and Schuster.

Gallas, A. (2017). Revisiting conjunctural marxism: Althusser and Poulantzas on the state. *Rethinking Marxism, 29*(2), 256–280.

Geoghegan, P. (2020). Cronyism and clientelism. *LRB*, 5 November. https://www.lrb.co.uk/the-paper/v42/n21/peter-geoghegan/cronyism-and-clientelism.

Gingrich, J. R. (2011). *Making markets in the welfare state: The politics of varying market reforms*. Cambridge University Press.

Gorton, S. (2021). Blog: Why the health and care bill is important. 15 September 2021 (Blog: Why the Health and Care Bill is so important | Article, Blogs | News | UNISON National) (Accessed 15 January 2022).

Greer, I. (2008a). Organized industrial relations in the information economy: The German automotive sector as a test case. *New Technology, Work and Employment, 23*(3), 181–196.

Greer, I. (2008b). Social movement unionism and social partnership in Germany: The case of Hamburg's hospitals. *Industrial Relations: A Journal of Economy and Society, 47*(4), 602–624.

Greer, I. (2016). Welfare reform, precarity and the re-commodification of labour. *Work, Employment and Society, 30*(1), 162–173.

Greer, I., Breidahl, K. N., Knuth, M., & Larsen, F. (2017). *The marketization of employment services: The dilemmas of Europe's work-first welfare states.* Oxford University Press.

Greer, I., Samaluk, B., & Umney, C. (2018b). Better strategies for herding cats. In *Reconstructing solidarity: Labour unions, precarious work, and the politics of institutional change in Europe* (166–187). Oxford University Press.

Greer, I., Samaluk, B., & Umney, C. (2019). Toward a precarious projectariat? Project dynamics in Slovenian and French social services. *Organization Studies, 40*(12), 1873–1895.

Greer, I., Schulten, T., & Böhlke, N. (2013). How does market making affect industrial relations? Evidence from eight German hospitals. *British Journal of Industrial Relations, 51*(2), 215–239.

Greer, I., Schulte, L., & Symon, G. (2018a). Creaming and parking in marketized employment services: An Anglo-German comparison. *Human Relations, 71*(11), 1427–1453.

Greer, I., Weaver, R., Belot, M., Lewis, E., Jautz, A., Kalmyka, Y., Rosin, M. & Branosky, N. (2021). *The new possible: Innovative workforce development and skills maps for Tompkins County.* Tompkins County Workforce Development Board.

Gregg, P. (2008). *Realising potential: A vision for personalised conditionality and support.* London: Department for Work and Pensions.

Grimaldi, A. & Pierru, F. (2020). L'hôpital, le jour d'après. *Le Monde Diplomatique.*

Guerrero, I., Mossé, P., & Rogers, G. (2009). Hospital investment policy in France: Pathways to efficiency and the efficiency of the pathways. *Health Policy, 93*(1), 35–40.

Hipp, L., & Warner, M. E. (2008). Market forces for the unemployed? Training vouchers in Germany and the USA. *Social Policy & Administration, 42*(1), 77–101.

Huws, U. (2021). Reaping the whirlwind: Digitalization, restructuring and mobilization in the Covid crisis. *Socialist Register 57*, 1–13.

Kołakowski, L. (2005). *Main currents of marxism* (2005 edition). Norton, 12–13.

Koukiadaki, A. (2014). The far-reaching implications of the Laval Quartet: The case of the UK living wage. *Industrial Law Journal, 43*(2), 91–121.

Krueger, A. B. (2019). *Rockonomics: A backstage tour of what the music industry can teach us about economics and life.* Broadway Business.

Kumar, A. (2020). *Monopsony capitalism: Power and production in the twilight of the sweatshop age*. Cambridge University Press.

Hall, P. (2018). Varieties of capitalism in light of the euro crisis. *Journal of European Public Policy, 25*(1), 7–30.

Hall, P., & Soskice, D. (2001). *Varieties of capitalism*. Oxford University Press.

Harvey, D. (2018). *A companion to Marx's capital: The complete edition*. Verso Books.

Hassink, R. (2005). How to unlock regional economies from path dependency? From learning region to learning cluster. *European Planning Studies, 13*(4), 521–535.

Hayek, F. A. (1980). *Individualism and economic order*. University of Chicago Press.

Heffer, S. (2020). Old-fashioned Protestant work ethic is Macron's plan. Blog *The Connexion*, 18 November 2020.

Hemmens, A. (2019). *Ne travaillez jamais. La critique du travail en France de Charles Fourier à Guy Debord*. Crise & Critique.

Hilferding, R. (1982). *Finance capital*. Routledge.

Höpner, M., Petring, A., Seikel, D., & Werner, B. (2011). Liberalisierungspolitik. *KZfSS Kölner Zeitschrift für Soziologie und Sozialpsychologie, 63*(1), 1–32.

Howell, C. (2016). Regulating class in the neoliberal era: The role of the state in the restructuring of work and employment relations. *Work, Employment and Society, 30*(4), 573–589.

Hürtgen, S. (2021). Precarization of work and employment in the light of competitive Europeanization and the fragmented and flexible regime of European production. *Capital & Class, 45*(1), 71–91.

Hutton, W. (2012). If Britain is to recover we must embrace new models of capitalism. *The Guardian*, 17 March 2012.

Jantz, B., Klenk, T., Larsen, F., & Wiggan, J. (2018). Marketization and varieties of accountability relationships in employment services: Comparing Denmark, Germany, and Great Britain. *Administration & Society, 50*(3), 321–345.

Jaehrling, K., Johnson, M., Larsen, T. P., Refslund, B., & Grimshaw, D. (2018). Tackling precarious work in public supply chains: A comparison of local government procurement policies in Denmark, Germany and the UK. *Work, Employment and Society, 32*(3), 546–563.

Johnson, M., Martínez Lucio, M., Grimshaw, D., & Watt, L. (2021). Swimming against the tide? Street-level bureaucrats and the limits to inclusive active labour market programmes in the UK. *Human Relations*.

Kohler-Hausmann, J. (2017). *Getting tough.* Princeton University Press.

Krachler, N., & Greer, I. (2015). When does marketization lead to privatisation? Profit-making in English health services after the 2012 Health and Social Care Act. *Social Science & Medicine, 124,* 215–223.

Krachler, N., Greer, I, & Umney, C. (2021). Can the public sector afford marketization? Market principles, mechanisms, and pushback in five health systems. *Public Administration Review.*

Lafargue, P. (1883). The right to be lazy. http://theanarchistlibrary.org/library/paul-lafargue-the-right-to-be-lazy

Lane, C. M. (2011). *A company of one.* Cornell University Press.

Lapavitsas, C. (2011). Theorizing financialization. *Work, Employment and Society, 25*(4), 611–626.

Lapavitsas, C. (2013). *Profiting without producing: How finance exploits us all.* Verso Books.

Laplane, A., & Mazzucato, M. (2020). Socializing the risks and rewards of public investments: Economic, policy, and legal issues. *Research Policy, 49*(2), 6.

Lazonick, W. & O'Sullivan, M. (2000). Maximizing shareholder value: A new ideology for corporate governance. *Economy and Society, 29*(1), 13–35.

Lee, T. L., & Tapia, M. (2021). Confronting race and other social identity erasures: The case for critical industrial relations theory. *ILR Review, 74*(3), 637–662.

Le Grand, J. (2003). *Motivation, agency, and public policy: Of knights and knaves, pawns and queens.* Oxford University Press.

Lethbridge, J. (2019). *Democratic professionalism in public services.* Policy Press.

Levy, J. D. (2008). From the dirigiste state to the social anaesthesia state: French economic policy in the longue durée. *Modern & Contemporary France, 16*(4), 417–435.

Leys, C. (2020). How market reforms made the NHS vulnerable to pandemics. *Tribune,* 24 March. https://tribunemag.co.uk/2020/03/how-market-reforms-made-the-nhs-vulnerable-to-pandemics

Lillie, N., & Greer, I. (2007). Industrial relations, migration, and neoliberal politics: The case of the European construction sector. *Politics & Society, 35*(4), 551–581.

Lipsky, M. (1980). *Street-level bureaucracy: Dilemmas of the individual in public service.* Russell Sage Foundation.

Lizé, W., Greer, I., & Umney, C. (2020). Artistic work intermediaries as industrial relations institutions: The case of musicians. *Economic and Industrial Democracy*. Online first.

Lødemel, I., & Moreira, A. (Eds.). (2014). *Activation or workfare? Governance and the neo-liberal convergence*. Oxford University Press.

London Evening Standard (2012). Iain Duncan Smith is the man to give the poor back their work ethic. *London Evening Standard*, 8 November 2014.

Machin, S. (2015). Real wage trends. Presentation at Understanding the Great Recession conference, Bank of England, September 2015.

MacLean, N. (2017). *Democracy in chains: The deep history of the radical right's stealth plan for America*. Penguin.

Madrigal, A. (2019). The servant economy. *The Atlantic*, 6 March 2019.

Malet, J. B. (2020). Derrière les murs de 'l'usine a colis'. *Le Monde Diplomatique*, April 2020.

Marchington, M., Willmott, H., Rubery, J., & Grimshaw, D. (Eds.). (2005). *Fragmenting work: Blurring organizational boundaries and disordering hierarchies*. Oxford University Press.

Marx, K. (1976). *Capital volume 1*. Penguin.

Marx, K. (1978). *Capital volume II*. Penguin Classics.

McCallum, J. K. (2020). *Worked over: How round-the-clock work is killing the American dream*. Basic Books.

McInroy, N. (2018). Wealth for all: Building new local economies. *Local Economy*, *33*(6), 678–687.

Miliband, R. (1969). *The state in capitalist society*. Basic Books.

Mirowski, P. (2013). *Never let a serious crisis go to waste: How neoliberalism survived the financial meltdown*. Verso Books.

Mirowski, P., & Plehwe, D. (Eds.). (2015). *The road from Mont Pèlerin: The making of the neoliberal thought collective, with a new preface*. Harvard University Press.

Mishra, P. (2020). Flailing states. *London Review of Books*, *42*(14). https://www.lrb.co.uk/the-paper/v42/n14/pankaj-mishra/flailing-states.

Moazed, A., & Johnson, N. L. (2016). *Modern monopolies: What it takes to dominate the 21st century economy*. St. Martin's Press.

Molloy, C. (2021). Forget the spin- the new English NHS bill is all about cutting our right to healthcare. *Open Democracy*, 13 July 2021.

Morgan, G., & Hauptmeier, M. (2021). The social organization of ideas in employment relations. *ILR Review*, *74*(3), 773–797.

Morton, A. J. (2021). European health care systems and the emerging influence of European Union competition policy. *Journal of Health Politics, Policy and Law, 46*(3), 467–486.

Mudge, S. L. (2008). What is neo-liberalism?. *Socio-Economic Review, 6*(4), 703–731.

National Audit Office. (2014). *The work programme.*

North, D. (1981). *Structure and change in economic history.* Norton.

Nozick, R. (1974). *Anarchy, state, and utopia.* Basic Books.

OECD (2008). *Growing unequal? Income distribution and poverty in OECD countries.* OECD.

O'Farrell, R., & Montagnier, P. (2019). Measuring digital platform-mediated workers. *New Technology, Work and Employment, 35*(1), 130–144.

Ozimek, A. (2012). Is Paul Krugman a free market guy? *Forbes,* 12 July 2012.

Paugam, S. (2002). *La société française et ses pauvres.* Presses universitaires de France.

PCS (2014). *Results of PCS membership survey on conditionality and sanctions.*

Perrenoud, M. (2006). Jouer «le jazz»: où, comment? Approche ethnographique et distinction des dispositifs de jeu. *Sociologie de l'Art, 1,* 25–42.

Peston, R. (2020). Has the furlough scheme removed the incentive to work? *Spectator,* 14 April 2020.

Peters, E. F., et al. (2005). The politics of path dependency: Political conflict in historical institutionalism. *The Journal of Politics, 67*(4), 1296.

Philippon, T. (2019). *The great reversal: How America gave up on free markets.* Harvard University Press.

Pierson, P. (2000). Increasing returns, path dependence, and the study of politics. *American Political Science Review, 94*(2), 251–267.

Piketty, T. (2014). *Capital in the twenty-first century.* Harvard University Press.

Pitts, H., & Bolton, M. (2018). *Corbynism: A critical approach.* Emerald.

Plehwe, D., Walpen, B., & Neunhöffer, G. (Eds.). (2007). *Neoliberal hegemony: A global critique.* Routledge.

Poulantzas, N. (2000). *State, power, socialism* (Vol. 29). Verso.

Pressley, A., & Stein, D. (2021). A federal job guarantee: The unfinished business of the civil rights movement. *The Nation,* 2 September 2021.

Refslund, B., Jaehrling, K., Johnson, M., Koukiadaki, A., Larsen, T. P., & Stiehm, C. (2020). Moving in and out of the shadow of European case law: The dynamics of public procurement in the Post-Post-Rüffert Era. *JCMS: Journal of Common Market Studies, 58*(5), 1165–1181.

Reuters (2012). Nicolas Sarkozy regrette d'avoir parlé du 'vrai travail'. *Reuters*, 26 April 2012.

Rothstein, B. (1998). *Just institutions matter: The moral and political logic of the universal welfare state*. Cambridge University Press.

Ruane, S. (2011). Save our hospital campaigns in England: Why do some hospital campaigns succeed? A preliminary exploration. Europe's Health for Sale. In J Lister (Ed.), *The Heavy Cost of Privatisation* (125–148) Libri Books.

Samaluk, B. (2017). Austerity stabilised through European funds: The impact on Slovenian welfare administration and provision. *Industrial Relations Journal, 48*(1), 56–71.

Sanson, D., & Courpasson, D. (2022). Resistance as a way of life: How a group of workers perpetuated insubordination to neoliberal management. *Organization Studies*. Online first.

Scharpf, F. (1999). *Governing in Europe: Effective and democratic?* Oxford University Press.

Schmalz, S., Ludwig, C., & Webster, E. (2018). The power resources approach: Developments and challenges. *Global Labour Journal, 9*(2), 113–134.

Schmid, G. (2008). *Full employment in Europe: Managing labour market transitions and risks*. Edward Elgar Publishing.

Schulte, L., Greer, I., Umney, C., Symon, G., & Iankova, K. (2018). Insertion as an alternative to workfare: Active labour-market schemes in the Parisian suburbs. *Journal of European Social Policy, 28*(4), 326–341.

Schwager, C. (2021). Kliniken werden geschlossen, obwohl das Gesundheitssystem vor dem Kollaps steht. *Berliner Zeitung*, 22 January 2021. https://www.berliner-zeitung.de/gesundheit-oekologie/kliniken -werden-geschlossen-obwohl-das-gesundheitssystem-vor-dem-kollaps -steht-li.132283

Sicot, D. (2020). Pas d'« argent magique » pour la santé » Le Monde Diplomatique, December 2020.

Silver, B. J. (2003). *Forces of labor: Workers' movements and globalization since 1870*. Cambridge University Press.

Sinclair, T. J. (1994). Passing judgement: Credit rating processes as regulatory mechanisms of governance in the emerging world order. *Review of International Political Economy, 1*(1), 133–159.

Skocpol, T. (1980). Political response to capitalist crisis: Neo-Marxist theories of the state and the case of the new deal. *Politics & Society, 10*(2), 155–201.

Soss, J., Fording, R. C., & Schram, S. F. (2011). *Disciplining the poor: Neoliberal paternalism and the persistent power of race.* University of Chicago Press.

Srnicek, N. (2017). *Platform capitalism.* Wiley.

Stettner, A. (2021). *7.5 million workers face devastating unemployment benefits cliff this labor day.* The Century Foundation.

Stiglitz, J. E. (2016). *The euro: How a common currency threatens the future of Europe.* WW Norton & Company.

Streeck, W., & Heinze, R. G. (1999). An Arbeit fehlt es nicht: die bisherige Beschäftigungspolitik ist gescheitert, eine radikale Wende unumgänglich: Im Dienstleistungssektor könnten Millionen neuer Arbeitsplätze entstehen. *Spiegel,* 10 May 1999, 38–50. https://www.spiegel.de/politik /an-arbeit-fehlt-es-nicht-a-23336b01-0002-0001-0000-000013220370 (Accessed 12 July 2021).

Streeck, W. & Thelen, K. (Eds.). (2005). *Beyond continuity: Institutional change in advanced political economies.* Oxford University Press.

Stockhammer, E., & Onaran, O. (2012). Rethinking wage policy in the face of the Euro crisis. Implications of the wage-led demand regime. *International Review of Applied Economics, 26*(2), 191–203.

Stockhammer, E., & Onaran, O. (2013). Wage-led growth: Theory, evidence, policy. *Review of Keynesian Economics, 1*(1), 61–78.

Stone, J. (2020). Coronavirus: Iain Duncan Smith says don't bring in universal basic income during the pandemic as it would be 'discincentive to work'. *Independent.* https://www.independent.co.uk/news/uk/politics/coronavirus -uk-update-universal-basic-income-iain-duncan-smith-a9411251.html.

Tcherneva, P. R. (2018). The job guarantee: Design, jobs, and implementation. *Levy Economics Institute, Working Papers Series,* 902.

Trappmann, V., Neumann, D., Umney, C., Joyce, S., Stuart, M. & Bessa, I. (2022). *Labour unrest during the pandemic. The case of hospital and retail workers in 90 countries.* International Labor Organization (in press at time of writing)

Umney, C. (2016). The labour market for jazz musicians in Paris and London: Formal regulation and informal norms. *Human Relations, 69*(3), 711–729.

Umney, C. (2017). Moral economy, intermediaries and intensified competition in the labour market for function musicians. *Work, Employment and Society, 31*(5), 834–850.

Umney, C., & Coderre-LaPalme, G. (2017). Blocked and new frontiers for trade unions: Contesting 'the meaning of work' in the creative and caring sectors. *British Journal of Industrial Relations, 55*(4), 859–878.

Umney, C., & Coderre-LaPalme, G. (2021). Marketization versus planning in neoliberal public services: Evidence from French hospitals. *Capital and Class*. Online first.

Umney, C., Greer, I., Onaran, Ö., & Symon, G. (2018). The state and class discipline: European labour market policy after the financial crisis. *Capital & Class, 42*(2), 333–351.

Umney, C., & Kretsos, L. (2014). Creative labour and collective interaction: The working lives of young jazz musicians in London. *Work, Employment and Society, 28*(4), 571–588.

Vidal, M. (2013). Postfordism as a dysfunctional accumulation regime: A comparative analysis of the USA, the UK and Germany. *Work, Employment and Society, 27*(3), 451–471.

Vincent, G. (2012). Partenariats public-privé, missions de service public, coopérations sanitaires: les limites du service public et du secteur public. In D. Tabuteau (Ed.), *Service public et santé Sciences Po* (89–96). Paris.

Vogel, S. K. (1998). *Freer markets, more rules: Regulatory reform in advanced industrial countries*. Cornell University Press.

Vogl, J. (2014). *The specter of capital*. Stanford University Press.

Wacquant, L. (2012). Three steps to a historical anthropology of actually existing neoliberalism. *Social anthropology, 20*(1), 66–79.

Warner, M. E., & Clifton, J. (2014). Marketisation, public services and the city: The potential for Polanyian counter movements. *Cambridge Journal of Regions, Economy and Society, 7*(1), 45–61.

Watkins, S. (2020). Politics in the pandemic. *New Left Review, 125*, 5–17.

Watts, B., Fitzpatrick, S., Bramley, G., & Watkins, D. (2014). *Welfare Sanctions and Conditionality in the UK*. Joseph Rowntree Foundation.

Webster, D. (2016). *Explaining the rise and fall of JSA and ESA sanctions 2010-16*. Report, Glasgow University, 3 October.

Webster, D. (2021). *Briefing: Benefit sanctions statistics*. University of Glasgow. November.

Wendling, A. (2009). *Karl Marx on technology and alienation*. Springer.

Wiggan, J. (2015). Reading active labour market policy politically: An autonomist analysis of Britain's work programme and mandatory work activity. *Critical Social Policy, 35*(3), 369–392.

Williams, E. (2021). Punitive welfare reform and claimant mental health: The impact of benefit sanctions on anxiety and depression. *Social Policy & Administration, 55*(1), 157–172.

Williamson, O. E. (1981). The economics of organization: The transaction cost approach. *American Journal of Sociology, 87*(3), 548–577.

Wills, T. (2021). In Berlin, overworked hospital staff went on strike for a month — and won. December 21. https://jacobinmag.com/2021/12/overwork-berlin-german-health-care-system-drg-strike-nurses-verdi-hospitals,

Zelizer, V. A. (1988). Beyond the polemics on the market: Establishing a theoretical and empirical agenda. *Sociological Forum, 3*(4), 614–634.

Index